DBT
SKILLS
FOR
TEENS
WITH
ANXIETY

DBT SKILLS

FOR

TEENS
WITH
ANXIETY

Practical Strategies to
Manage Stress & Strengthen
Emotional Resilience

Atara Hiller, PsyD

ZEITGEIST • NEW YORK

Published in the United States by Z Young Adult, an imprint of Zeitgeist™,
a division of Penguin Random House LLC, New York.

penguinrandomhouse.com

Zeitgeist™ is a trademark of Penguin Random House LLC

ISBN: 9780593435960
Ebook ISBN: 9780593690437

Art © by Bibadash/Shutterstock.com
Author photograph © by Alycia Hinrichsen
Edited by Clara Song Lee

Book design by Aimee Fleck

Printed in the United States of America

1st Printing

First Edition

To the many teens I've treated with DBT over the years. Your commitment to building a life worth living, despite the obstacles in your way, inspires me to keep doing this challenging and incredibly fulfilling work.

CONTENTS

How This Book Can Help

Over the past 30 years, dialectical behavior therapy (DBT) has helped millions of adults, teens, and children learn to manage their emotions more effectively.

If you are reading this book, you have likely been struggling with anxiety. You might be feeling stressed and overwhelmed, experiencing panic attacks, avoiding certain places or situations, struggling with other anxiety-related symptoms, or all of the above. Whatever your stress and anxiety look like, the DBT skills in this book can help you gain control of your emotions so they don't control you!

This book will teach you how to:

- Cope with stressful situations, such as relationship conflicts, exams and essays, job interviews, the college application process, and everyday life problems
- Make wise and effective choices even amid strong emotions
- Focus more easily

- Experience emotions without acting on them in problematic ways
- Identify and work toward short- and long-term goals
- Build more positive experiences
- Reduce your risk of negative emotions by maintaining your physical well-being
- Communicate better
- Think about and respond to situations more flexibly
- Overcome rejection and failures and increase self-esteem and self-compassion

Keep a separate notebook for doing the exercises and activities in this book. That way, if there is anything in this book that you want to show your parent, caregiver, or anyone else in your life, they won't see your private thoughts.

Although the teenage years can be tough, your future is unwritten and full of potential. With DBT, you can break free from chronic stress and anxiety and move forward with greater peace.

Introduction

DBT BASICS

Dialectical behavior therapy (DBT) is an effective treatment for people who struggle with emotions, including anxiety, depression, anger, and shame. DBT was developed by a psychologist named Marsha Linehan, and it is an evidence-based treatment, meaning that there has been a lot of research showing it is helpful, for people with borderline personality disorder (BPD). BPD is characterized by chronic difficulties with thoughts, emotions, behaviors, identity, and relationships with others. People with BPD often struggle with other problems, including anxiety. DBT is shown to help treat these difficulties in adults and teens, even if they don't have BPD.

What makes DBT so helpful? For many people, it's the DBT skills, which teach people to control their emotions and manage their lives more effectively. In fact, DBT includes five modules of life skills that can be particularly helpful if you are often stressed:

MINDFULNESS—helps us stay present in the moment, which is often less stressful than what we are worrying about!

DISTRESS TOLERANCE—helps us cope with difficult situations without responding in a way that makes things harder for us in the long term.

EMOTION REGULATION—helps us reduce the likelihood that we will experience intense emotions and allows us to decrease unwanted intense emotions after they start.

INTERPERSONAL EFFECTIVENESS—helps us be more successful in our interactions with others so we're more likely to get what we want, build and maintain relationships, and feel good about ourselves!

WALKING THE MIDDLE PATH helps us think and feel more flexibly and be more open-minded about situations so we can be more effective in dealing with them.

I personally find DBT skills to be incredibly helpful and studied the works of Dr. Linehan, Dr. Jill Rathus, and Dr. Alex Miller, who adapted DBT to treat adolescents, so I could share DBT with my clients. As a licensed psychologist, I exclusively use DBT to treat teens and young adults who struggle with their emotions, and I train other mental health professionals on how to provide DBT. In all my years of doing DBT, I've seen it dramatically change people's lives for the better!

I worked with one teen who struggled with severe social anxiety. She was constantly worried about what people thought of her, how to talk to people, and whether she said the wrong thing when she did speak. She also yearned for a major role in her school's annual theater performance but had always been too anxious to try out. By learning and utilizing various DBT skills, she learned to control her emotions and worry thoughts more effectively and was able to focus more on her schoolwork, develop meaningful friendships with confidence, and, most impressively, steal the show in a leading role in her school's play.

Another teen had a hard time focusing on anything because she was always worrying about something: the health of her family, current events, upcoming tests, or friends being mad at her. DBT skills helped her rein in her distress so it didn't consume her and also enabled her to focus more on her goals and relationships than on her worries.

For serious or persistent anxiety, there are comprehensive adolescent DBT programs, but they generally require a minimum of six months of individual and group therapy. However, even the DBT skills in this book can help you manage your stress at home.

As a teenager, you have a lot to manage, like schoolwork, extracurricular activities, jobs, and relationships. When you're struggling with anxiety, it makes all of those things even harder and more exhausting. But taking the time and energy to learn and practice these skills can make your life a lot easier and more enjoyable without the burden of chronic stress and anxiety weighing you down.

PART ONE

DBT SKILL SETS

The next five chapters will introduce DBT skill sets based on the five modules you read about on pages 10-11. Each chapter includes various activities you can do to practice the skills and add them to your coping toolbox. The more you practice the skills, the easier they will become to implement whenever you need them!

The material in these chapters is based on the work of Marsha Linehan, PhD; and Alec Miller, PhD and Jill Rathus, PhD, who adapted DBT for adolescents. The skills and their descriptions have been tailored to focus on teens with anxiety, and they've been made more approachable for people who can't access a DBT therapist right now. The skills are listed in a particular order for a reason, and feel free to read and use this book in a way that works for you! Please don't feel bound to read this book in the order provided.

Chapter One

SEE CLEARLY WITH MINDFULNESS

When we feel anxious and stressed, we're often thinking about the past or worrying about the future. Mindfulness helps us stay present in the moment *right now*. By slowing down and being aware of our current thoughts, emotions, sensations, and urges without judging them, you can respond thoughtfully rather than impulsively. Mindfulness skills are the foundation for all the other skills in this book because, as Dr. Linehan astutely observed when developing DBT, you need mindfulness to identify what you're feeling and why. If you aren't aware of what's causing your distress, you can't use skills to deal with it. Let's get mindful!

MINDFULNESS SKILLS IN ACTION

Olivia's mind was always filled with negative self-judgments, resulting in chronic stress and headaches. To stop the constant negative thinking, Olivia learned to mindfully observe her thoughts and notice when she treated a negative thought like a fact. When Olivia saw pictures of her friends hanging out without her, she caught herself thinking,

They must not like me. Instead of believing this thought, she reframed it as *I'm having the thought that no one likes me.* This approach helped Olivia react differently and, in turn, feel more positive about herself. She used other DBT skills to ask her friends about the pictures. It turns out there was a valid reason why she was not included.

Elijah struggled with procrastination. For a long time, he attributed this behavior to being lazy. Recently, he learned to mindfully observe and describe his current emotions, physical sensations, urges, and the facts of the situation without judgment. When he failed to generate a list of colleges to consider, he automatically decided it was because he was lazy. Mindfulness taught him to observe: *I'm feeling overwhelmed because I don't know what I want to do with my life. I'm avoiding the task so I don't need to think about it.* By describing the facts of the current situation, he could figure out how to get the task completed instead of avoiding it.

In both examples, what was happening in the present was less problematic and more solvable once the facts became the center focus and the judgments were removed. By practicing mindfulness, you can access your Wise Mind, a concept developed by Dr. Linehan that refers to the ability to integrate your emotions, logic, and reason to a situation so you can do whatever is in the best interest of your goals.

WHERE YOU ARE NOW

According to DBT, mindfulness is very helpful for controlling your mind and, as a result, gaining more control over your emotions, actions, and life. Discover how mindful you are by answering these questions in your DBT journal or notebook. After some mindfulness practice, reassess yourself and see how much progress you've made!

- Do you act on autopilot; for example, going from point A to point B without remembering how you got there?

- When you socialize with family or friends, do you space out or think about other stuff?

- When you're engaging in pleasurable activities, do you spend that time thinking about other stuff?

- Do you do multiple things at once, like eating while watching TV or doing homework or talking to a friend while texting with someone else?

- When doing homework, do you get distracted by other thoughts?

- Do you say or do things without realizing you were going to do it, like yell at someone or blurt something out?

If you answered yes to even some of these questions, the following mindfulness practices will help! Research shows that just 10 minutes of mindfulness practice a day can help people control their emotions more effectively.

MINDFULNESS
OF ACTIVITIES
Wherever you go, there you are

(Adapted from Linehan, 2015; Rathus and Miller, 2015)

> ## WHAT YOU'LL NEED
>
> ● A watch or timer
>
> ● Whatever you need to do an activity of your choice. It can be anything: brushing your teeth or hair, taking a walk, playing an instrument or a sports activity.

Mindfulness may conjure up images of Buddhist monks meditating on top of a mountain. DBT invites us to focus on living a mindful life, where we practice mindfulness in our day-to-day activities and experiences to reap its benefits. Here are two options for practicing mindfulness to get you started.

INSTRUCTIONS

Option #1: Observing and describing an activity

1. Set your watch or timer for 2 minutes.

2. Use your senses to notice what's happening while you engage in your chosen activity. What do you see, smell, hear, taste, and feel?

3. Describe whatever you're noticing without judgment, and stick to the facts. For example, "I taste mint from my toothpaste," "I smell grass and see pink flowers blooming on a tree," "I feel bumps on an orange basketball."

4. If you notice your attention wandering, bring your attention back to your senses.

Option #2: Participating in an activity

1. Set your watch or timer for 2 minutes.
2. Fully engage in the activity of your choice. Let go of any self-consciousness or judgment, and immerse yourself in whatever you're doing.
3. If you notice your attention wandering, or judgments popping into your head bring your attention back to fully participating in the activity of the present moment.

TAKEAWAYS

How was that experience for you? Was it more enjoyable or interesting than in the past? How did you feel? Less anxious? Were you focused the whole time, or did your mind wander? Could you bring your attention back? If so, you were practicing mindfulness successfully! As you can see, opportunities for mindfulness can be found anywhere anytime. When you increase the mindful moments in your life, you can reduce emotional suffering and experience more pleasure and greater well-being.

5-4-3-2-1
Grounding yourself with your senses

WHAT YOU'LL NEED

● Something to eat or drink (optional)

When we panic, we can lose touch with the present and get caught up in our fears and bodily sensations. This can feel scary! In these situations, ground yourself in the present moment and get out of your body and your head. It's great because it can be done anytime, anywhere, and for as long as you need to do it.

INSTRUCTIONS

1. Observe **5** things you can see that you hadn't noticed before. *Examples: the picture on a wall, your hands, the color of a book, clouds in the sky*

2. Notice **4** things you can feel with your hands or body. *Examples: the sensations of your butt on a chair, your feet on the ground, your hands clasped, a soft blanket, a furry pet*

3. Listen for **3** things you can hear. Expand your awareness to sounds you might not normally hear. *Examples: your breath, a clock ticking, a car horn, an air conditioner humming*

4. Notice **2** things you can smell. These can be pleasant and unpleasant smells on or around you. *Examples: shampoo, perfume, coffee, garbage*

5. Notice **1** thing you can taste. If nothing is available to you, what tastes are in your mouth? Or open your mouth and taste the air.

TAKEAWAYS

Were you successful in shifting your attention from internal sensations, thoughts, and emotions to these external sensations? Are you feeling a little more grounded? Less anxious? Did you focus on things you hadn't previously noticed? This mindfulness practice is a great example of how expanding your awareness of the present moment can help you feel less anxious or at least more in control right now. This window of control frees you to make the next effective or "wise" choice.

MINDFULNESS OF URGES
Urge surfing

WHAT YOU'LL NEED

- A watch or timer
- A comfortable space to sit or lie down where you won't be disturbed

Oftentimes when we feel anxious and stressed, we have urges to engage in behaviors that could get in the way of achieving our long-term goals. Unhealthy urges might include skipping school or practice, avoiding friends, self-injuring, using alcohol or drugs, or engaging in a disordered eating behavior. Acting on these urges might bring relief in the short term, but they can cause problems for you in the long term. Being aware of your urges and learning not to act on them are useful skills to help you regain control of your body and your life.

INSTRUCTIONS

1. Set your watch or timer for 2 minutes.
2. Notice any urges in your body: *the urge to move, scratch an itch, blink your eyes, or something else.*
3. Instead of acting on each urge, simply notice and describe it without judgment. *For example, "I have the urge to move my legs." "I have the urge to swallow."*

(Adapted from Linehan, 2015; Rathus and Miller, 2015)

4. If you do act on an urge, do it with awareness. *For example, "I'm choosing to blink my eyes right now."*

5. If you notice your attention wandering, bring your attention back to noticing and describing your urges as they come and go, increase and decrease, and finally go away.

TAKEAWAYS

Was it possible for you to notice urges and *not* act on them? If you did act on urges, could you do it intentionally rather than impulsively? And if so, how did it feel? Once you're comfortable with this practice, feel free to challenge yourself by practicing it with more challenging urges that happen in response to your emotions. The key is to step back and notice how the urge evolves over time with curiosity rather than reactivity. With time and practice, you can break the connection in your brain between urge and action so you can experience an urge without acting on or judging it.

MINDFULNESS OF THOUGHTS
You are not your thoughts!

> **WHAT YOU'LL NEED**
> - A timer (optional)
> - A piece of paper or your DBT journal (optional)
> - A pen or pencil (optional)

This exercise will help you learn that thoughts are not facts; they are simply neural firings in the brain that we can't necessarily control. The goal isn't to empty our minds of thoughts; instead, it's to change our relationship with them. By labeling our thoughts as just thoughts, we can separate them from ourselves and our identities. Mindfulness of Thoughts helps us respond better to whatever situation is generating those thoughts and allows us to feel better about ourselves in the process.

NOTE: Try option #1 first, then try option #2 once you're comfortable with the first exercise. You also can do option #2 in your head without writing down every thought. There does not need to be a time limit. Do it as long as it's necessary to be helpful.

INSTRUCTIONS

Option #1: Writing down every thought

1. Set your timer for 2 minutes.

2. Write down every thought that pops into your head. It can be anything—even the thought *I have no thoughts in my head right now*. Notice worry thoughts, assumptions, catastrophizing thoughts, "shoulds." If the same thought keeps coming back, keep writing it down.

3. If you find your attention wandering, bring your attention back to noticing and writing down your thoughts.

Option #2: Describing your thoughts

1. Notice your thoughts as they come and go, like waves in the ocean ebbing and flowing.

2. Describe each thought as a thought. *Examples: There's the thought that this is too hard. There's the thought that I can't think of anything. There's the thought that I need to be perfect.*

3. Try not to get stuck on a thought or caught up in believing it. Don't push it away, block it, or try to change it. Simply acknowledge its presence without judging it as good/bad, right/wrong, true/false, fair/unfair, should/shouldn't be happening.

4. Get curious about your thoughts. Ask yourself, *How did these thoughts come about?* Notice that every thought that has entered your mind has also left it.

5. Remember, you aren't your thoughts. You don't need to act on them.

6. If you notice your attention wandering, bring your attention back to noticing and describing your thoughts.

(Adapted from Linehan, 2015; Rathus and Miller, 2015)

TAKEAWAYS

How did your thoughts feel to you when you described them this
way? Did they feel less factual? Did you feel less attached to them?
Negative thinking and worry thoughts often contribute to our stress
and anxiety. Learning to recognize our thoughts as simply thoughts
helps us be less attached to them and instead see our circumstances
for what they are and *not* what we *think* they are. By observing our
thoughts coming and going without judgment, showing curiosity
toward our thoughts, and recognizing that we are not our thoughts, we
can feel more compassion for ourselves and others, which enhances
our self-esteem.

MINDFULNESS OF GRATITUDE
Finding the good

WHAT YOU'LL NEED

- A piece of paper or your DBT journal
- A pen or pencil
- A comfortable space where you won't be disturbed

When we are feeling stressed and anxious, it can be challenging to see what's going well in our lives. Mindfulness can be helpful when we are feeling negative or neutral emotions and want to feel positive ones like happiness, satisfaction, and contentment. A regular mindfulness practice of gratitude will help increase your sense of well-being, which can help you weather the storm of stressors in a more effective way.

INSTRUCTIONS

1. Write down at least three things that went well today and for which you are grateful.
2. Next to each experience, write why this positive event happened.

TAKEAWAYS

How did it feel to focus on the positive experiences in your life? Do you feel a greater sense of satisfaction or contentment? The goal with this mindfulness practice is not to ignore or downplay the challenges in your life. Rather, it's about recognizing that we have a choice of what we focus on in the present moment, and this impacts our mood and actions. When we focus on what's going well or even what's *not* going poorly, and express gratitude for those things, our anxiety decreases. Practice this every night, and see what happens!

ACCESSING YOUR WISE MIND

WHAT YOU'LL NEED

● A comfortable space where you won't be disturbed

Wise Mind is the wisdom within us. It's the synthesis of our emotions and reason that allows us to make effective choices. Ever have a gut feeling or hunch about something or know something intuitively? That's your Wise Mind. We all have one. Sometimes, though, our Wise Mind might be blocked by strong emotions, urges, or a purely logical mind-set that can elicit a false sense of certainty and wisdom. We need to sift through those layers to access our Wise Mind. This mindfulness practice will help you access your Wise Mind. When you do, you will feel a sense of peace and contentment.

INSTRUCTIONS

1. Get into a comfortable position and close your eyes. Place your hands on your lap, palms facing up.

2. Breathing in normally, say to yourself, *Wise*. Focus all of your attention on the word.

3. Breathing out normally, say to yourself, *Mind*. Focus all of your attention on the word.

4. Repeat as necessary until you sense that you have settled into Wise Mind.

5. If you notice your mind wandering from your breath and the words, gently bring your attention back.

(Adapted from Linehan, 2015)

TAKEAWAYS

When we feel calm, it can be easier to access our Wise Mind. When we are feeling stressed and anxious, it's more challenging. What was your emotional state during this practice? How did it affect the time it took and ability to access your Wise Mind? If it was difficult, try practicing this exercise frequently when you're feeling more relaxed. Practice may make it easier to access your Wise Mind during a stressful situation so you can successfully call upon your Wise Mind superpower to help you make effective choices.

WHERE YOU HOPE TO BE SOON

Now that you've learned about and experienced the benefits of mindfulness, take some time to journal about how mindfulness might help you. Identify up to three ways that you can bring more mindfulness into your daily life. What are things you do regularly that you can do more mindfully? Which mindfulness exercises in this book were helpful? Which ones do you want to improve? Check out the mindfulness resources in the back of the book (page 173), or create your own. Remember that mindfulness generally involves the following three steps:

1. Choose something to focus on. Remember, it can be anything—an object, activity, or the words of another person, or something internal, like thoughts, emotions, sensations, or urges.

2. Focus. Observe, describe, or fully participate in it without judgment or attachment.

3. Refocus as needed. When your attention wanders (which happens!), notice that this has happened and gently bring your attention back.

Begin slowly. Start off with 30-second mindfulness practice intervals, and work your way up to 1 minute, 2 minutes, and beyond. You can practice mindfulness anytime and anywhere. Remember, the goal of mindfulness is the practice itself: paying attention on purpose to this moment right now.

(Adapted from Rathus and Miller, 2015)

Chapter Two

STRENGTHEN YOUR DISTRESS TOLERANCE

When we're feeling stressed, we may do things that make our situation worse, such as skip school or spend hours on TikTok in avoidance. Dr. Linehan included Distress Tolerance skills in DBT to help us cope with difficult circumstances and avoid doing things that could create more challenges in the long term. If you can't solve a problem or change how you feel about a situation right now, use these skills. You'll know they are working, not by feeling better, but by not doing anything to make things worse.

DISTRESS TOLERANCE SKILLS IN ACTION

Rachel's chronic medical condition often got in the way of her ability to attend classes, participate in extracurricular activities, and hang out with friends. She felt frustrated and stressed about her situation and feared for her health (understandably!). She used harmful behaviors to cope, which led to more challenges. Rachel then learned to practice Distress Tolerance skills to decrease the intensity of the physical sensations of her emotions, distract from and soothe her physical pain, and accept the problems her medical condition caused. These skills helped her do the best she could, given the circumstances.

Ranya felt anger, fear, and sadness over current events and worried about the future. Unmotivated to engage in any productive behaviors, she thought, *What's the point?* She began practicing Radical Acceptance of the situations and her emotions, distracted herself from the pain of these situations, and focused on finding meaning in these events. As a result, she didn't do anything that could make things worse for her personally.

These examples highlight some painful experiences that teens face and cannot always avoid. Often, our emotions cause us to act impulsively to satisfy short-term needs, such as avoiding or escaping these painful situations. However, if we live our lives this way, we become miserable, hurt ourselves and others, and still don't get what we want. Distress Tolerance skills offer another option: tolerating and accepting the pain.

WHERE YOU ARE NOW

Take out your DBT journal and list five strategies you use when you feel distressed. What are examples of these strategies, what are possible outcomes or consequences when using these strategies, and are they helpful? To evaluate the strengths and weaknesses of each strategy, you can create a table that looks similar to this example:

STRATEGY	EXAMPLES	POSSIBLE OUTCOMES	IS THIS STRATEGY HELPFUL? (YES/NO/SOMETIMES)
Ruminating/ dwelling	Constantly thinking about a breakup or failing a test and how awful it is	Keeps my mind on *why* something happened, which I can't change, instead of what I *can* do about it, which I can control	No; it just keeps me stuck.
Talking to someone about my problems	Calling my friends to vent when I'm upset about my parents	Feels better when it's helpful and feels worse when it isn't; sometimes creates drama because of gossip	Sometimes— depends on who I talk to. Some people are better at helping me feel better than others.

Were you able to list five strategies? Are most of them helpful? Whatever your responses were, by the end of this chapter, you'll discover new strategies (or rethink current ones!) that may help you cope with distressing situations more easily.

DISTRACT YOURSELF WITH ACCEPTS

> **WHAT YOU'LL NEED**
> - A piece of paper or your DBT journal
> - A pen or pencil
> - Whatever you need for one of the suggested activities

One way to help us tolerate difficult situations (without doing something to make it worse) is by distracting ourselves. The acronym ACCEPTS is a helpful way to remember different ways we can distract ourselves. You can either choose one you've used before, or try something new and see if it helps. Here are some suggestions:

A CTIVITIES: Engage in a nonstressful activity.

Examples: Read a book, talk to someone, watch TV or videos, take a walk, listen to music, draw, or paint.

C ONTRIBUTIONS: Be kind to someone.

Examples: Hug someone, do a favor, complete chores without being asked, help someone with homework, write a gratitude letter, volunteer, donate money or items.

C OMPARISONS: Compare yourself to people who are worse off than you are or times when you were doing worse. (And don't invalidate yourself by saying, "So, I shouldn't be feeling X because it could be worse.")

(Adapted from Linehan, 2015; Rathus and Miller, 2015)

E M O T I O N S : Engage in activities that elicit different emotions than you're feeling.

Examples: If you're feeling sad, watch something funny or dance; if you're feeling angry or anxious, listen to calming music.

P U S H A W A Y : Temporarily push your problems out of your mind.

Examples: Visualize putting your problems in a box on a high shelf in the farthest closet; think about or do something else instead.

T H O U G H T S : Fill your head with other thoughts.

Examples: Read, sing songs, do puzzles, count.

S E N S A T I O N S : Distract yourself with other physical sensations.

Examples: Blast music, take a hot/cold shower, splash cold water on your face, chew or hold ice, squeeze a stress ball, cuddle in a blanket, do crunches.

INSTRUCTIONS

1. In your DBT journal, write down the time.
2. Choose two ACCEPTS strategies from the list above, and mindfully participate in them as long as you wish.
3. Upon completion of each activity, write down the time and ask yourself the following question: *Did the skill help me tolerate distressing emotions and/or urges without doing something to make things worse while I engaged in the activity?*
4. If yes, congratulate yourself! If no, try again with another skill from this exercise. It's okay for not every skill to work for everyone and/or to need multiple skills to tolerate a painful situation!

TAKEAWAYS

Hopefully, by doing this exercise, you were sufficiently distracted so you could resist the urge to act on your emotions. Remember, the goal of these strategies isn't to help you feel better or solve the problem— it's just to pass a little time in a healthier way—so if you're still feeling distressed or stressed about a problem, that's understandable. Later in this book, you'll find skills designed to help reduce negative emotions and solve problems. Remember, if you *didn't make things worse*, then you were successful with this exercise!

SELF-SOOTHE WITH YOUR SENSES

WHAT YOU'LL NEED

- Your DBT journal or a piece of paper
- A pen or pencil
- Anything you need to engage some or all of your senses

When we're feeling stressed and overwhelmed, it can feel like a mini getaway when we surround ourselves with pleasant sensory experiences! The key is to engage in these activities mindfully so our attention is focused on the soothing experience. Here are some ideas:

VISION

Examples: Look at pleasant pictures, notice the colors outside your window, people-watch, shake a glitter jar and watch it settle.

HEARING

Examples: Listen to your favorite music, nature sounds (outside or online), or a podcast; sing or play a musical instrument.

SMELL

Examples: Smell your favorite lotion, body wash, or shampoo; smell yummy food; smell flowers or other things in nature.

TASTE

Examples: Savor a cozy food and/or drink.

TOUCH

Examples: Cuddle with something soft, take a shower or bath, hug someone (or yourself), play with slime or finger paint.

(Adapted from Linehan, 2015; Rathus and Miller, 2015)

INSTRUCTIONS

1. In your DBT journal or on a piece of paper, write down the time.

2. Choose two Self-Soothing strategies from the list above, and mindfully participate in them as long as you wish.

3. Upon completion of each activity, write down the time and answer the following question: *Did the skill help me tolerate distressing emotions and/or urges without doing something to make things worse?*

4. If yes, congratulate yourself! If no, try again with another skill from this exercise. Different skills work for different people!

TAKEAWAYS

How was your mini getaway? Did it distract you from your problems? If you noticed your mind wandering, that's okay. Hopefully, you brought your attention back to the activity. Did you have thoughts that you didn't deserve to engage in such a soothing activity while you had so much stress or "more important" things to do? That's normal, too! Remember, you're using these skills because your emotions are getting in the way of tackling those problems. Self-soothing gives you the space to calm down in a comforting way. Remind yourself what's in your long-term best interests—sometimes it's taking the time for a little self-love!

IMPROVE THE MOMENT

> ## WHAT YOU'LL NEED
> - Your DBT journal or a piece of paper
> - A pen or pencil
> - Anything you need to use the suggested strategies

IMPROVE skills can help you tolerate difficult situations by creating positive experiences in the midst of the challenges you're facing. They are particularly helpful when a stressful situation seems never ending or when distractions with ACCEPTS and Self-Soothing strategies aren't working. You don't usually need any props for this activity. Here are some suggestions:

IMAGERY: Imagine a relaxing or confidence-inducing scene. Use all your senses.

MEANING: Identify a positive aspect of the painful situation. Ask yourself: *Did anything positive come out of this difficult situation?*

PRAYER: Appeal to God, a higher power, or your own Wise Mind, and ask for the power to tolerate the pain.

RELAXATION: Relax your muscles by listening to a relaxation recording, stretching, or taking a bath. Use progressive muscle relaxation (page 49).

(Adapted from Linehan, 2015; Rathus and Miller, 2015)

ONE THING IN THE MOMENT: Focus all your attention on what you're doing. Observe your physical sensations, and notice what's going on around you.

VACATION: Give yourself a break from the stress. Go outside, take a walk, plan a day trip, unplug, read something.

ENCOURAGEMENT: Talk to yourself like you would a dear friend. Repeat statements like *I can get through this. I can tolerate this. I'm doing my best. This won't last forever.*

INSTRUCTIONS

1. In your DBT journal or on a piece of paper, write down the time.
2. Choose two IMPROVE strategies from the list above, and mindfully participate in them for as long as you wish.
3. Upon completion of each activity, write down the time, and answer the following question: *Did the skill help me tolerate distressing emotions and/or urges without doing something to make things worse?*
4. If yes, congratulate yourself! If no, try again with another skill from this exercise.

TAKEAWAYS

Were you focused on the images or activities of these skills? Did it help improve your immediate situation while you were engaging in the skill? Were you distracted from your stress and anxiety enough to avoid acting on your emotions and/or urges? If you noticed your mind wandering back to the distressing situation, that's okay as long as you could bring your attention back to the activity. The goal of these strategies isn't to help you solve the problem but to help you avoid making your circumstances worse. If you didn't make things worse, then you used these skills effectively! And if you are still feeling distressed or stressed about a problem, check out the skills in the later chapters to help.

PROS AND CONS OF TOLERATING URGES AND DIFFICULT SITUATIONS

WHAT YOU'LL NEED

- Your DBT journal or a piece of paper
- A pen or pencil
- A comfortable space where you won't be disturbed

Have you ever made a list of pros and cons? This one is a little different. In DBT, listing Pros and Cons is a Distress Tolerance skill. The content generally needs to be completed when you are in a Wise Mind state. Then, when you are distressed, you can read what you wrote in Wise Mind and be reminded of your resolution to tolerate your distress and not act on urges.

INSTRUCTIONS

1. Identify a behavior you use when you are distressed that causes problems for you and that you would like to stop. It might be engaging in a harmful or addictive behavior, escaping or avoiding, or giving up or giving in to something.

2. Create a large chart in your DBT journal or on paper that looks like the one on page 46.

3. Fill out the boxes in order from A to D. Think about the impact on yourself (your motivation, emotions, physical body, self-esteem, thoughts), your relationships and other people, and your future:

    a. List the pros, or benefits, of acting on the urge. Why do you do it?

    b. List the cons, or downsides, of acting on the urge. Why shouldn't you do it? How does it cause problems for you?

    c. List the cons of not acting on the urge and using skills instead. Why is it so hard not to act on the urge? To use skills?

    d. List the pros of not acting on the urge and using skills instead. What are the benefits of using skills and not engaging in the behavior?

4. Review each item listed in each box, and determine whether it's a short-term (ST) or long-term (LT) consequence/issue/benefit, or both (ST/LT).

5. Underneath the table, write your Wise Mind conclusion based on the information collected.

6. When the urge arises to engage in the behavior, review your pros and cons. Feel free to take a screenshot so you have access to it on your phone.

(Adapted from Linehan, 2015; Rathus and Miller, 2015)

	PROS	CONS
Acting on urge and engaging in behavior (write the specific behavior)	A	B
Resisting the urge and using skills instead	D	C

TAKEAWAYS

Did you notice that the pros of acting on urges and cons of resisting the urges tend to be shorter term, and refraining from engaging in the behavior and using skills has more long-term benefits (in addition to short-term benefits)? Seeing all this information written on paper can help you make a Wise Mind choice. Once you're comfortable with doing this strategy on paper, you can also do it in the moment when unexpected urges arise. By doing so, you can access your Wise Mind and let it help you tolerate your urges and distress instead of acting on them ineffectively.

TIPP SKILLS FOR INTENSE EMOTIONS

WHAT YOU'LL NEED

- A comfortable space where you won't be disturbed

FOR OPTION #1:

- A timer (optional)

- A heart rate monitor (optional)

- A piece of paper (optional)

- A pen or pencil (optional)

- Any one of the following: a bowl of cold water, a sink filled with ice-cold water, a cold pack, two ice packs, two frozen water bottles, or two sandwich bags filled with ice cubes

When feeling intense emotions, it can be hard to think straight, use skills, and make wise choices. These TIPP skills are incredibly easy and useful strategies to calm the body and decrease emotional arousal. The skills create these results by changing your body chemistry, so they work outside your willingness for them to work (as long as you at least do them!). They work fast! If your body is physically calmer, you will feel calmer, which will allow you to use other skills to cope effectively with your stress.

NOTE: If you have any medical issues, please consult with your doctor before using options #1 or #2.

INSTRUCTIONS

Choose from the following options:

Option #1: **Temperature cool-down**

1. Optional first step: Measure your heart rate. Either use the heart rate monitor or check your pulse. To do so, put your pointer and middle finger on the front side of your neck below your jawbone until you feel a pulse. Count how many beats you feel in 15 seconds, and multiply that number by 4 to calculate your heart rate. (You can also take your pulse on your wrist.) Otherwise, skip this step, and go on to step 2.

2. Take a deep breath and hold.

3. Bend down and dunk your face into cold water (in the bowl or sink) OR bend down and place the ice on your cheekbones and eyes. Hold for 30 seconds or as long as you can.

4. Repeat steps 2 and 3 three times.

Option #2: **Intense exercise**

1. Choose an aerobic exercise, such as walking fast, running, jumping jacks, jumping rope, or dancing.

2. Engage in the exercise for a short while, ideally at least 10 minutes.

Option #3: **Paced breathing**

1. Focus on your breath, and breathe deeply into your abdomen to a count of 4.

(Adapted from Linehan, 2015; Rathus and Miller, 2015)

2. Breathe out slowly to a count of 6 or 8.

3. Repeat for 1 to 2 minutes until your breathing has slowed and you are feeling calmer. The key element is breathing out more slowly and for longer than breathing in.

Option #4: Progressive muscle relaxation

1. Get into a comfortable position sitting or lying down.

2. Tense and release any or all of the following muscle groups. Notice the tension, and hold for 10 seconds. Release for at least 10 seconds, noticing the relaxation flowing through that area. Repeat each muscle group once.

   a. Tense your face by closing your eyes and scrunching your forehead and nose together. Release.

   b. Tense your lower face and jaw by biting down and scrunching up your lips and nose toward your eyes. Release.

   c. Tense your neck and shoulders by tightening your neck and raising your shoulders high. Release.

   d. Tense your back by arching back and bringing your shoulder blades together. Release.

   e. Tense your chest by taking a deep breath and holding it. Let go when it becomes difficult.

   f. Tense your arms and hands by making tight fists and bending both arms up to touch your shoulders and squeezing. Release.

   g. Tense your abdomen by holding in your stomach tightly. Release.

h. Tense your legs by extending them in front of you, squeezing your thighs together, and flexing your feet toward you. Release.

i. Tense your ankles and feet by extending your legs in front of you, curling your toes under, and flexing your feet toward you. Release.

3. Scan your body for any remaining tension, and let that tension go.

4. Relax for 1 minute, focusing your attention on your breath.

NOTE: When you are in a public setting, focus on the muscle areas causing the most tension in your body. It may be helpful to record yourself reading this script so you can listen to it whenever you want to guide yourself through this exercise.

TAKEAWAYS

Did you feel calmer quickly? Try all of these strategies, and see which ones work best for you. You might find that some work better in one setting—maybe paced breathing works better in public settings, while temperature works better at home. The important thing to remember about TIPP skills is that while they work fast, the calming effects don't last long—10 to 20 minutes max. So, you'll want to use the other skills in this chapter and book to help you continue managing your anxiety effectively. We'll talk more in chapter 6 about how to put all the skills together.

TURNING THE MIND
Practicing Radical Acceptance

WHAT YOU'LL NEED

- Your DBT journal or a piece of paper
- A pen or pencil
- A comfortable space where you won't be disturbed

Our life can be spent wishing for someone or something to be different or for something we don't have. If only we had different parents, a more attractive body, a romantic partner, more money to buy (insert heart's desire here), or were smarter/funnier/more talented/and so on in some way! In DBT, Radical Acceptance means seeing reality for what it is and acknowledging the things in our life that we can't change right now, along with any disappointment we might feel. It's radical because we need to practice it all the way: we need to think it, feel it, and act like it. We don't have to like our reality; we also don't need to be passive or forgive. Rather, if we can't solve a problem, Radical Acceptance is a useful tool to prevent us from making a painful situation even worse. Why does this work? Because denying reality doesn't change reality, and changing your reality requires accepting it first! Sometimes, we can't change our circumstances right away, so we need to tolerate the discomfort, at least in the short term, to avoid getting stuck in misery and making things worse.

INSTRUCTIONS

1. Notice that you are denying the reality of something in your life. This is something that you can't solve right now, and your feelings fit the facts for the situation. You might feel tension in your body when you think about it or think judgments about it. (*This shouldn't be happening. This isn't fair. This is wrong.*) Write it down.

2. Make an inner commitment to accept this situation. Remember, you don't have to like it or approve of it; you just need to recognize that this situation is in your life right now. Write down what radical acceptance looks like for you with regard to this situation. What would you do differently if you accepted your reality instead of rejecting it?

3. Think about your situation, and turn your mind from rejecting to accepting your reality. Do this as often as possible, even if your mind feels like a Ping-Pong ball.

4. Choose from the following exercises to help you turn your mind toward radical acceptance. They communicate to your brain to take a more accepting stance. Practice one while you think about the situation.

    a. Half-smile: Relax your facial muscles. Lift the tips of your lips ever so slightly—barely noticeably.

    b. Willing hands: Face your palms up on your lap. Relax your hands.

    c. Mindfulness of your breath: Observe the sensations of air flowing into your nose, through your body, and back out.

(Adapted from Linehan, 2015; Rathus and Miller, 2015)

d.   Remember your choice: Remind yourself that acceptance is a choice you have in a situation that feels out of your control.

e.   Picture it: Review what you wrote, and imagine what radical acceptance would look like in this situation.

5.   Write down your experience using these strategies. Were you able to radically accept your situation at least in the moment? How did it affect your emotions, thoughts, and physical sensations to move from rejecting reality to accepting reality?

TAKEAWAYS

Practicing radical acceptance is hard work! Do you notice how you have to keep turning your mind toward acceptance? Radical acceptance is definitely not something you do once and then you are done. It's a process that happens over and over again; hopefully, with time, it gets easier or the situation changes, and there's nothing that needs accepting anymore. While radical acceptance can be challenging, the alternative is staying miserable or making choices that make your circumstances even more challenging. Wouldn't you rather invest your energy into making life more manageable rather than making it more miserable? So, please keep practicing radical acceptance and turning the mind. It'll be worth it!

WHERE YOU HOPE
TO BE SOON

The Distress Tolerance skills that you learned in this chapter are not permanent solutions to your problems, but sometimes temporary solutions like these are needed in the short term to help you be effective in coping with difficult situations. Just be mindful that you don't use them too frequently, since doing so could cause you to avoid or resist dealing with your anxiety and the situations that are causing it. You need to use the skills in the other chapters of this book too!

Now that you've learned a bunch of new coping skills, go back to your original list of coping strategies that you created at the start of the chapter (page 35). Do you have any ideas for improving your coping tool kit? Feel free to create a new chart, or you can mark up your chart, crossing out strategies that don't work for you, adjusting skills you use, and adding strategies from this chapter that you have found helpful. Also note any new strategies that you would like to try!

Chapter Three

MANAGE YOUR EMOTIONS SKILLFULLY

When we feel stressed, anxious, and afraid, it can feel like these emotions will never end. However, we can't just snap our fingers and make them disappear. Our emotions are always prompted by something, whether it's external—like an argument, a failed test, or something we saw or heard—or internal—like a memory, thought, or physical sensation. In this chapter, you'll learn strategies to decrease the intensity of emotions so they don't continue to cause problems for you. You'll also learn how to decrease the likelihood of experiencing these emotions in the first place. You won't have to remain stuck in the endless cycle of these painful emotions!

EMOTIONAL REGULATION SKILLS IN ACTION

Sumin has an important test coming up—the outcome will have a big impact on her future. She's so worried about the test that she avoids preparing for it, thinking that she's just going to do poorly anyway. As it gets closer, Sumin becomes even more anxious and starts cramming for it, but she feels like nothing is sticking in her head. She considers skipping the test. But then she chooses to use her Emotion Regulation skills to check the facts on her emotions and problem-solve how she could effectively prepare for the exam with the time left. She also uses the skills to plan how to be effective the day of the exam, which ends up going well.

Alex struggles with body image despite all the support they get from their friends. So, they hide their body beneath baggy clothes. When Alex gets invited to go swimming with their friends, they want to decline. However, Alex uses Emotion Regulation skills to act opposite to those urges and instead comes up with a plan to go swimming in a way that is comfortable for them.

Both these examples illustrate how we can experience emotions, thoughts, and urges, which can be valid based on past or current experiences. Yet just because we are feeling a certain way and have particular urges, doesn't mean we need to act on them. In fact, what we do in response to those emotions and urges can decrease those emotions and urges, making it easier to achieve our goals. While it can be challenging to retrain our brain when it's used to thinking, feeling, and responding a certain way, it can be done—with practice!

WHERE YOU ARE NOW

Emotion regulation is the ability to identify your emotions and control when and how you experience and express them. Take out your DBT journal, and write about your current strengths and weaknesses when it comes to managing your emotions.

- Do you experience intense emotions?

- Can you specifically label your emotions?

- Are you aware of what makes you more susceptible to experiencing intense emotions?

- Do you take actions to reduce these vulnerabilities?

- Can you stop unwanted emotions once they start?

- What strategies do you use to stop these unwanted emotions?

- Do these tactics help you or make things worse?

EMOTION IDENTIFICATION
What's my emotion?

WHAT YOU'LL NEED

- A piece of paper or your DBT journal
- A pen or pencil
- A comfortable space where you won't be disturbed

Often, we label our emotions as "I felt bad/good" or "I'm upset." However, research shows that being able to accurately label our emotions increases our emotion regulation capabilities. Think about it: If we can accurately define the problem, we can solve it more effectively. If we go to the doctor and say, "My body hurts," it'll be harder for the doctor to identify the solution versus if we say, "I fell on my wrist yesterday, and now it's painful and swollen." This exercise will help you increase your emotion identification abilities.

INSTRUCTIONS

1. Make a copy of the chart on pages 60–61 in your DBT journal or on a piece of paper.
2. Read the content, and fill in the blank spaces with specific times when you felt each emotion.

What was it like to label your experiences with specific emotion words? Emotions can feel scary or aversive to people, yet emotions serve multiple purposes. They are a form of communication to ourselves and others. The urges that come from emotions also make it easier for us to respond quickly and effectively in situations. Emotions also give us information about what's going on in our environment (although not always accurately!). If we identify and take charge of our emotions, they can actually be helpful to us. So, continue practicing identifying your emotions as different situations arise. See how you can feel more in control just by naming them!

BASIC EMOTION	JUSTIFIABLE REASONS
Fear, anxiety	There is a threat to your life, health, or well-being or that of someone you care about.
Anger	A desired goal or activity is blocked; you or someone you care about is hurt in some way.
Sadness	You've experienced a loss, whether of a person, pet, or thing, or a loss in expectations/hopes/ wants.
Shame	You fear rejection if something about you is revealed.
Guilt	Your behaviors go against your values or morals.
Disgust	You come in contact with something contaminating or poisonous; a disliked individual is touching you or someone you care about; you are around others who can negatively influence you or the group you are part of.
Envy	You want what someone else has.
Jealousy	There is a threat that an important relationship or object will be damaged, lost, or taken from you.
Love	Something or someone enhances your or another's quality of life and/or helps you achieve your goals.
Happiness	You experience pleasure, satisfaction, enjoyment, or contentment with your current situation.
Surprise	Something unexpected occurs.
Curiosity/ interest	You want to get to know someone or something.

	EXAMPLE OF A TIME YOU FELT THIS WAY

Adapted from Emotion Regulation Handout 8a in *DBT Skills Training Handouts and Worksheets* by Marsha Linehan (2015)

ABC PLEASE SKILLS

Most people engage in daily dental hygiene to prevent cavities. The ABC PLEASE skills are *emotional* hygiene practices that reduce our vulnerability to intense emotions and their consequences. Just like we wouldn't wait to take care of our teeth until after we have cavities, it's not wise to wait to take care of emotions until an emotional crisis arises. The ABC PLEASE skills are a collection of smaller activities that we can do regularly to reduce our vulnerabilities. Dr. Linehan developed the acronym ABC PLEASE as a helpful way to remember all the ways you can achieve this purpose:

ACCUMULATING SHORT- AND LONG-TERM POSITIVE EXPERIENCES

BUILDING MASTERY

COPING AHEAD

PLEASE SKILLS

- Treat **P**hysica**L** illness.
- Balance **E**ating.
- **A**void mood-altering drugs.
- Balance **S**leep.
- Get **E**xercise.

All of these skills are covered in this chapter, except for the Cope-Ahead strategy, which is discussed in chapter 6 (pages 135–136).

ABC PLEASE
Accumulating Short-Term Positive Experiences

WHAT YOU'LL NEED

- Activities of your choice, based on the instructions below
- A piece of paper or your DBT journal
- A pen or pencil

Can you think of a time when something difficult happened to you on a "good" day? Now, think of a time when something similar happened to you on a "bad" day. If you noticed that you reacted differently, it's likely because you had fewer or more vulnerabilities, depending on the day. Engaging in more positive experiences on a regular basis will set the stage for more "good" days, making it easier to deal with the challenges that arise in life.

INSTRUCTIONS

1. Write down one pleasant activity to do today.
2. Before you engage in the activity, rate your mood on a scale of 0 to 5, with 0 being very distressed and 5 being great.
3. Fully engage and participate in the activity, even if you aren't in the mood. Focus all of your attention on it. If your mind wanders, bring your attention back to the activity.

(Adapted from Rathus and Miller, 2015)

4. Once you've completed the activity, rate your mood again on a scale of 0 to 5. Did you notice a difference in your mood?

5. Repeat at least once a day!

TAKEAWAYS

How did you feel before you engaged in the pleasant activity versus afterward? Did your mood improve? You may notice that if you engage in a pleasant activity once in a while, it won't have a major impact on your life. The key here is doing so on a regular basis, even if you don't feel like it. It's even more beneficial if you engage in different kinds of activities on a regular basis. There might be things in life you don't enjoy doing that you do regularly anyway because you "have to" (for example, go to school or work, complete chores, keep doctor appointments). Why not prescribe yourself daily pleasant experiences, too, as a way to reduce your stress and anxiety?

ABC PLEASE
Accumulating Long-Term Positive Experiences

> **WHAT YOU'LL NEED**
> - A piece of paper or your DBT journal
> - A pen or pencil

One way to reduce our vulnerabilities to negative emotions is by taking steps toward fulfilling long-term goals. These goals include doing things that fit our personal values and developing positive and lasting relationships. If we take action steps toward our future, it'll help make the stress along the way easier and more worth it and will reduce our stress long term as we make important positive changes in our lives.

INSTRUCTIONS

1. Identify one long-term goal that *you* (not your parents, friends, or community) want to achieve in life. Write it down, being as specific as possible.

2. Break down and list the steps you need to take toward achieving that goal.

3. Avoid avoiding. Put a star next to the first next step that you need to take, and then go do it!

4. Write about how you felt engaging in this step toward your long-term goal. Did you notice a difference in your mood?

5. Continue taking the next steps toward your long-term goal.

(Adapted from Linehan, 2015; Rathus and Miller, 2015)

TAKEAWAYS

Hopefully, you felt accomplished taking the first or next step toward your long-term goal! If it was difficult, try breaking the steps down even more. Did the following kinds of thoughts burden you in any way: *It shouldn't be so hard to do this* or *Anyone can do this . . . why is it such a big deal that I did it?* That's normal, especially among people who struggle with anxiety and depression. Remind yourself that if the task was so easy, you would have done it already. You are doing the best you can, and this is something you can work toward doing even better! Also, use your Mindfulness of Thoughts skills (page 25) to notice the judgments and let it go, bringing your attention back to the activity.

ABC PLEASE
Building Mastery

WHAT YOU'LL NEED

- A piece of paper or your DBT journal
- A pen or pencil

According to Drs. Linehan, Miller, and Rathus, another way to reduce our vulnerabilities is to engage in activities that build mastery or allow us to feel capable, accomplished, and in control of our lives. Activities that build mastery are challenging but possible and include tasks that we *need* to do—like completing homework, chores, or work obligations—and activities that we *want* to do—like practicing a hobby, learning a new skill, or working on a project. Building mastery can involve completing small tasks that have been nagging at you, or it can involve more complex activities that help you go from where you are now to where you want to be in the future (such as getting a tutor or signing up for lessons in something you want to get better at). A blend of daily pleasant *and* mastery-building activities is a great way to build resilience against the stress in your life and increase your self-esteem , confidence, and overall happiness!

INSTRUCTIONS

1. List three things you can do to challenge yourself, get better at something, or check something off your to-do list. Choose activities that are difficult *and* possible.

2. Choose one and do it. If you find it's too difficult, do something easier.

3. Write down how it felt to engage in the activity. Did you feel masterful? Accomplished? On the right track? Effective? In control?

TAKEAWAYS

As you continue engaging in activities that build mastery, try gradually increasing the challenge of the task. After all, if you want to learn to play piano, practicing "Mary Had a Little Lamb" all the time will get boring. If you keep challenging yourself, you will grow to feel more confident and competent, an effective buffer against negative experiences and emotions.

(Adapted from Linehan, 2015; Rathus and Miller, 2015)

ABC PLEASE
PLEASE skills

> **WHAT YOU'LL NEED**
> - A piece of paper or your DBT journal
> - A pen or pencil

The PLEASE skills allow us to care for our emotional well-being and reduce our vulnerabilities to negative emotions by caring for our physical well-being. Can you think of times when you were tired, hungry, or sick; maybe drunk or high; or sat in bed all weekend, and you reacted more intensely to a situation? That makes sense—our physical health has a big impact on our mood and ability to regulate ourselves. Use this activity to take stock of your lifestyle choices and identify what you can do differently to improve your physical well-being. Making changes will not only reduce your emotional vulnerabilities but will also improve your health, giving you less to worry about! These are the PLEASE skills:

TREAT **P**HYSICAL I**L**LNESS: Take medications as prescribed, see a doctor if necessary, slow down when you are sick.

BALANCE **E**ATING: Eat a variety of foods and nutrients. Don't eat too little or too much. Avoid foods that make you feel emotional.

(Adapted from Linehan, 2015; Rathus and Miller, 2015)

AVOID MOOD-ALTERING DRUGS: Don't use nonprescribed drugs and alcohol. Remember that caffeine and nicotine are also mood-altering.

BALANCE **S**LEEP: Get the amount of sleep you need to feel rested. Maintain a regular bedtime routine and schedule.

GET **E**XERCISE: Move your body throughout the day.

INSTRUCTIONS

1. Identify one of the above skills to practice today.
2. Practice it, even if you aren't in the mood.
3. Write about your experience. Did you notice a difference in your mood? How about in your responses to situations as they arose?

TAKEAWAYS

Making changes to your physical well-being isn't always easy. If it was so simple to get enough hours of sleep a night or exercise, we would all be doing it all the time! To see the benefits of this skill, it's important to do it consistently. You might not immediately feel the positive results; they'll build up over time.

CHECK THE FACTS
Are my feelings justified?

> **WHAT YOU'LL NEED**
> - A piece of paper or your DBT journal
> - A pen or pencil
> - A comfortable space where you won't be disturbed

You hang out with your friend every day after school, and one day, she doesn't show up. You may think to yourself, *Is she mad at me? What did I do wrong?* and feel confused, sad, scared, guilty, or angry. Those thoughts and emotions might lead you to avoid, ignore, text her non-stop, and/or lash out. Later, you learn that she had a family emergency and her phone died, so she couldn't contact you. This new information likely changes the way you think and feel about the situation, which, in turn, affects your behavior. Check the Facts helps us determine whether our emotional reactions fit the facts of the situation.

INSTRUCTIONS

1. Think of a situation that is causing painful emotions.
2. Write down one emotion you want to change. How intensely are you feeling this emotion on a scale of 0 to 100 (0 being no distress and 100 being the most distressed)? How long have you been feeling this way?

(Adapted from Linehan, 2015; Rathus and Miller, 2015)

3. Write down the situation that is causing the emotion, as if you were talking to a friend.

4. Separate fact from interpretations/assumptions/judgments by asking yourself (write down your responses):

   a. Am I correctly interpreting the situation? Are there other possible explanations? What is the most likely interpretation?

   b. Am I thinking about the situation in extremes; for example, catastrophizing (*she hates me*), all-or-nothing thinking (*this always happens to me*), "should" statements (*I should have been a better friend*)?

   c. What is the worst that I am imagining, and what are the chances of that happening?

   d. Even if the worst-case scenario did occur, how can I cope well with it?

5. Based on all the information gleaned in step 4, does the emotion and/or intensity and/or duration fit the actual facts? Write down whether the emotion still fits, and if it does, note any changes in the intensity or duration.

TAKEAWAYS

How'd this exercise go for you? You might have realized that (a) the emotion doesn't fit the facts, and the newfound knowledge could decrease the emotion almost immediately; (b) the emotion doesn't fit the facts, but the emotion is still sticking around, and you need additional help in making it go away; (c) the emotion does fit the facts, but the intensity and/or duration does not, so you may or may not need

(Adapted from Linehan, 2015; Rathus and Miller, 2015)

further assistance in translating that from your brain into action; or (d) the emotion and its intensity and duration do indeed fit the facts, in which case you're stuck with a painful experience about which you may want to do something. The good news is that the next few exercises will help with all these potential outcomes!

NOTE: If you found this skill challenging, perhaps you are feeling intense emotions right now that are getting in the way of using the logic and reason this skill requires. If so, use the Distress Tolerance skills in chapter 2 first to bring down the intensity a bit, or practice this on a less emotionally upsetting situation first.

PROBLEM-SOLVING DIFFICULT SITUATIONS

WHAT YOU'LL NEED

- A piece of paper or your DBT journal
- A pen or pencil
- A comfortable space where you won't be disturbed

So, maybe you've checked the facts (pages 71–72) on a painful situation and determined that your emotions do fit the facts. If you want to stop feeling those painful emotions, one option is to do something about the event causing the emotions. If there is no more prompting event, you won't feel the emotion anymore! Problem-Solving is a helpful Emotion Regulation strategy to help change an event or solve a problem that is causing painful emotions.

INSTRUCTIONS

1. Think of a situation or event that is causing painful emotions.
2. Write down one emotion you want to change. How intensely are you feeling this emotion on a scale of 0 to 100? How long have you been feeling this way?
3. Write down a description of the situation causing the emotion.
4. Use the Check the Facts skill (pages 71–72) to be sure you have a problem situation. If your emotion fits the facts, the situation is a problem, and your Wise Mind says it is effective to act on this

(Adapted from Linehan, 2015; Rathus and Miller, 2015)

emotion, continue this exercise. If it doesn't fit the facts, Check the Facts might be enough, or use the Opposite Action (page 77) or Wave Skill (page 84).

5. Write down your goal in solving this problem. What needs to happen for you to feel better? Keep your goal simple and realistic.

6. Brainstorm and list at least three solutions. You can even ask others for suggestions. Don't evaluate your solutions; just list them. Let your mind go wild generating ideas!

7. Choose the solution that is most likely to achieve your goal. If unsure, choose the two best solutions, and use Pros and Cons to compare them and decide which one to try first. You can use the table on page 76 to guide you.

8. Try the solution you chose.

9. Evaluate the outcome. Write down your answer to the following question: *Did the solution solve my problem and make it go away?*

10. If yes, congratulate yourself! If no, congratulate yourself for trying and don't give up. Go back to step 6, and identify another solution to implement. Keep trying new ideas until you're successful.

TAKEAWAYS

When we feel strong emotions, we often want to make the problem go away as quickly as possible. If we react immediately, we risk making ineffective choices. If we give ourselves the time and space to solve our problems, it's incredibly helpful in reducing and eliminating negative emotions effectively.

NOTE: If you had difficulty completing this exercise because you were feeling intense emotions, you might need to first tolerate and decrease them with the skills in Chapter 2. If you were problem-solving on your own and struggled to find solutions, perhaps reach out to people you trust to help. It's normal for our first attempt at problem-solving not to work—keep trying, and you'll get there!

	SOLUTION 1:	SOLUTION 2:
Pros		
Cons		

OPPOSITE ACTION

WHAT YOU'LL NEED

- A piece of paper or your DBT journal
- A pen or pencil
- A comfortable space where you won't be disturbed

If you've checked the facts and determined that either (1) your emotion doesn't fit the facts, but you are still feeling it and want it to go away, or (2) your emotion fits the facts, but it's not effective for you to act on that emotion, you can use Opposite Action. Opposite Action is a helpful Emotion Regulation skill where, by changing your behaviors, your emotion will decrease or go away. Every emotion is associated with an urge. Acting on that urge maintains that emotion; engaging in behaviors that counter that urge will change the emotion. Opposite Action isn't a quick fix; it can take up to 45 minutes to work. You also need to do it *all the way*; your thoughts, body chemistry, facial expressions, body posture, and behaviors need to be consistent with acting opposite to the urges of the emotions you want to change. If you keep doing Opposite Action all the way, your emotion will change and you will feel more in control!

INSTRUCTIONS

1. Write down one emotion that you want to change.
2. Write down the specific urges that you have as a result of that emotion (see chart, pages 80–83, for examples).

(Adapted from Linehan, 2015; Rathus and Miller, 2015)

3. Ask yourself:
   - *Does the emotion fit the facts of the situation?*
   - *If yes, will acting on the urges be effective?*
   - *Will it help me or make things worse?*
4. If your emotion doesn't fit the facts and/or acting on the urge won't be effective, continue with opposite action.
5. Using the chart on pages 80–83 as a guide, write down what an opposite action would look like for you in this situation, asking yourself:
   - *What behaviors do I need to engage in?*
   - *What thoughts should go through my mind?*
   - *What should my facial expressions and body posture be like?*
   - *How can I change my body chemistry to be consistent (see TIPP on page 47)?*
6. Engage in the opposite action all the way! Focus all your attention on the activity. If your mind wanders to negative things, bring your attention back to the Opposite Action exercise. Keep doing it until your emotion reduces enough for you to notice.
7. Come back and write about your experience. How did you feel after acting opposite to your emotion?

TAKEAWAYS

Opposite Action is hard work! It requires us to accept our emotions and deal with them directly instead of avoiding or escaping them. The good news is it's an effective strategy for decreasing emotions and dealing with urges that are causing problems for us. Think about it: We don't become confident public speakers by avoiding public speaking. Instead, we create change by doing things differently.

NOTE: If you didn't notice a difference, ask yourself if you really did it all the way. Were your thoughts, facial expressions, body posture, and/or body chemistry consistent with Opposite Action? Did you give your presentation but think the whole time you were going to fail and mumble through it? Did you get out of bed and show up for a pleasant activity but think the whole time that you didn't want to be doing it and not fully engage in it? Also, consider whether the emotion to which you were acting opposite was the primary emotion causing your distress. Sometimes, anger masks fear, sadness, or shame—if so, try targeting those emotions instead.

Opposite Action Chart

EMOTION	URGES
Fear, Anxiety	Escape, avoid
Sadness	Withdraw, isolate, become passive
Anger	Attack, fight
Shame	Hide, avoid, withdraw, try to appease others, attack others as a way to protect yourself

OPPOSITE ACTION

Approach what you are afraid of over and over until your fear decreases to where it fits the facts.

Get active—engage in pleasant activities and build mastery.

1. Gently avoid the person with whom you are angry AND/OR
2. Be kind. Take a step back, and think about what's going on for the other person. Build sympathy/empathy even if you don't agree.

Share your personal characteristics/behaviors with supportive people; repeat the behavior that elicits shame around people who won't reject you; don't apologize for a perceived mistake; stand proud and maintain eye contact.

Note: If shame does not fit the facts/isn't effective but guilt does/is:

1. Share your behavior with people who won't reject you.
2. Apologize.
3. Fix what broke as a result of your actions
4. Commit to not making the mistake again and work to prevent it from happening again.
5. Accept the consequences.
6. Recognize what made this behavior happen, and forgive yourself.
7. Let it go!

Adapted from Emotion Regulation Handout 11 in *DBT Skills Training Handouts and Worksheets* by Marsha Linehan (2015) and Emotion Regulation Handout 20 in *DBT Skills Manual for Adolescents* by Jill Rathus and Alec Miller (2015)

Opposite Action Chart (Cont.)

EMOTION	URGES
Guilt	Hide, beg for forgiveness, overpromise that you won't offend again, deny all responsibility
Jealousy	Control, accuse, "snoop," act suspicious
Disgust	Avoid, escape, push away, treat someone/something with disrespect
Love	Say "I love you" and give affection, want to and spend time with someone, do what the other person wants/needs

OPPOSITE ACTION

Share your personal characteristics/behaviors with supportive people; repeat the behavior that elicits guilt around people who won't reject you; don't apologize for a perceived mistake; stand proud and maintain eye contact.

Note: If guilt does not fit the facts/isn't effective but shame does:

1. Hide your actions if you want to stay in that group.
2. Use your interpersonal skills (see chapter 4) and work to change the person's/group's values.
3. Validate yourself (see chapter 5).

OR

1. Join a new group that fits your values and won't reject you.
2. Repeat the behavior that elicits guilt with your new group.
3. Validate yourself (see chapter 5).

Let go of controlling other people's actions, stop snooping, relax your body and face.

1. Approach.
2. Be kind—think about what's going on for the other person that could be contributing to their behavior. Build sympathy/empathy (even if you don't agree with it!).

Stop expressing love by avoiding the person and distracting yourself from thinking about that person.

WAVE SKILL
Mindfulness of emotions

WHAT YOU'LL NEED

- A watch or timer
- A piece of paper or your DBT journal
- A pen or pencil
- An emotional song, video, or scene in a book, movie, or TV show (optional)
- A comfortable space where you won't be disturbed

Believe it or not, the average emotion lasts 90 seconds. Yet, emotions can be like Velcro, resulting in emotions sticking around longer! When we experience an emotion, memories of other times when we felt that way, judgments about that emotion, and worry thoughts about the future of that emotion can attach themselves to the initial emotion, making the emotional experience so much more intense and longer in duration. As a result, emotions seem to last forever! However, when we experience intense emotions that we don't like and fit the facts, the most effective thing to do is allow ourselves to experience them and give them the time to fizzle out on their own. Drs. Rathus and Miller's Wave Skill teaches us that emotions are valid, and they come and go on their own like waves in an ocean. By welcoming and accepting them, we can tolerate them until they disappear, which helps them go away more quickly and completely.

INSTRUCTIONS

1. Note the time you are starting this exercise.

2. Cue an emotionally evocative song, video, or scene in a book, movie, or TV show OR practice this when you are feeling a negative emotion that fits the facts.

3. Focusing your attention on just one emotion, allow yourself to experience that emotion. Step back and notice it. Don't try to hold on to it or push it away. Allow yourself to experience the emotion as a wave, ebbing and flowing, coming and going.

4. Notice the physical sensations this emotion elicits and where you feel those sensations in your body. Experience them fully. If thoughts about your emotion or the experience that elicited the emotion come to mind, bring your attention back to the physical sensations.

5. Remind yourself that you are not your emotion, and you don't need to act on the emotion. Think of times when you felt differently than you do now.

6. Radically accept that the emotion is part of you. Let go of judgments about the emotion.

7. Repeat steps 3 to 6 until the emotion has passed. Note the time.

(Adapted from Linehan, 2015; Rathus and Miller, 2015)

TAKEAWAYS

When we feel emotions, our tendency is often to suppress them, run away from them, or attempt to fix the problem eliciting the emotion as quickly as possible. However, we know those first two options aren't effective in the long run, and we can't always fix the problem. What was it like being mindful of your emotion, welcoming it into your awareness, accepting it, and letting it run its course without attaching more to it? Hopefully, you realized that emotions don't need to be catastrophic experiences avoided at all costs. With time, practicing the Wave Skill when your emotions fit the facts can help you feel less misery and more freedom and control.

WHERE YOU HOPE TO BE SOON

By using the Emotion Regulation skills in this chapter, you are taking a significant step toward regulating your emotions more effectively so you have the control over your life (or at least your emotions!) you desire. Now that you've learned how to manage your emotions better, review the Emotion Regulation strengths and weaknesses you identified on page 58. Take some time now to respond to the questions I asked you earlier, and write how one or more skills you have learned in this chapter have helped or can help strengthen your ability to manage intense emotions. The goal is that with continued practice of these strategies, you can have a life where you respond to challenges with more calm and ease.

Chapter Four

PRACTICE USEFUL INTERPERSONAL SKILLS

Interactions with family, friends, romantic partners, and even random strangers can be a cause of stress and anxiety. Furthermore, when we are stressed all the time, it can take a toll on our relationships with others and how we communicate with them. Dr. Linehan developed the Interpersonal Effectiveness skills in DBT to give us the tools to be more effective in our relationships by helping us get what we want from other people, build and strengthen positive relationships and end problematic ones, and build and maintain our self-respect!

INTERPERSONAL SKILLS IN ACTION

Jamal is really struggling in math. He feels uncomfortable asking for help. He realizes that if he continues avoiding talking to his teacher, he'll fail the class and have to attend summer school. Instead, Jamal acts opposite to his fear and shame and uses his Interpersonal Effectiveness skills to ask his teacher for additional support. His teacher agrees to help him.

Masami is worried about a friend and the behaviors in which she is engaging, but she is scared to say anything because she's worried her friend will get angry at her. Masami realizes that her concern for her friend outweighs her fears for the consequences of speaking up. She uses her Interpersonal Effectiveness skills to express her concerns and listen to what her friend has to say. At first, the friend is angry that Masami is saying anything, but when Masami continues to use her Interpersonal Effectiveness skills, the friend calms down. The friendship remains intact, and their bond is strengthened due to Masami's nonjudgmental support.

Both these examples highlight the challenges that can occur in relationships. We may not have the skills to manage them; additionally, emotions, worry thoughts, and/or indecisiveness can get in the way of being effective. However, the skills you'll learn in this chapter will help you successfully navigate all kinds of relationships now and far beyond your teenage years!

WHERE YOU ARE NOW

Pull out your DBT journal, and take a few minutes to write about your current strengths and weaknesses when it comes to communication and managing relationships. Are relationships stressful for you? How do you handle conflict? How comfortable are you asking for things or saying no to something you don't want to do? Do people get frustrated with you for not paying attention, or do they feel like you listen? When someone says something that makes you feel uncomfortable, do you speak up? Are you quick to judge and make assumptions about people, or do you give the benefit of the doubt to others? This information will help you understand your current strengths and opportunities for growth.

ASSERT YOURSELF
WITH DEAR MAN

WHAT YOU'LL NEED

- A piece of paper or your DBT journal
- A pen or pencil
- A comfortable space where you won't be disturbed
- The person with whom you need to talk

Have you ever wanted or needed someone to do something for you but felt too scared to ask? Has anyone ever asked you to do something for them that you didn't want to do, but you felt too uncomfortable to say no? Even if you did ask for or say no to something, did it not go well because you were too aggressive (yelling, blaming) or too passive (not being clear with your needs)? DEAR MAN skills (page 94) are interpersonal effectiveness skills to help you assert yourself effectively and increase the likelihood that you'll get what you want from others! The acronym, DEAR MAN, is a helpful way to remember what to say and how to say it.

INSTRUCTIONS

1. Write about an upcoming situation where you need to ask someone for something or need to say no to someone.

2. Think about your priorities in this situation. In any interpersonal situation, you can have one of three priorities:

(Adapted from Linehan, 2015; Rathus and Miller, 2015)

a. Obtaining your objective: getting what you want/saying no to something you don't want to do

b. Building or maintaining a relationship

c. Maintaining your self-respect

If your #1 priority is obtaining an objective, proceed with the next steps. If building or maintaining the relationship and/or maintaining your self-respect is important, too, read about the GIVE and FAST skills on pages 97 and 100, which you'll need to incorporate into your DEAR MAN.

3. Think about the following factors to determine if and when it's appropriate to make your request of the other person or say no, and how intensely to do so. Write down your responses and your decision based on your responses:

CAPABILITIES: Is the person capable of giving you what you want, or do you have what the person wants?

TIMELINESS: Is this a good time to ask/say no?

PREPARATION: Do you have all the facts? Are you sure about what you want?

RELATIONSHIP: Is what you want, or what the person is asking of you, appropriate to the relationship?

GIVE AND TAKE: Has the other person helped you before? Has the other person helped you too much already? Have you helped the other person before? Have you helped the other person too much already?

RIGHTS: Does the law or morals obligate the person to give you what you want, or are you obligated to give what the person wants?

AUTHORITY: Are you in charge of the other person, or are they in charge of you? Is that person asking for something within their authority?

LONG-TERM VERSUS SHORT-TERM GOALS: Will your request/response maintain the peace now but cause problems later? Which is more important, the current state of the relationship or the long-term?

4. Based on your responses to step 3, use the DEAR MAN skill to write down what you will say to that person (see page 94).

5. Practice your DEAR MAN so it feels comfortable to speak. If you are going to email/text your DEAR MAN to someone, finalize the email/text.

6. Go and do your DEAR MAN!

7. Come back and write about your experience. What was the result?

TAKEAWAYS

Did you feel more comfortable asserting yourself, knowing that you had a structure to guide you? Hopefully, you were successful in achieving your outcome! If you weren't, did you follow all the steps? Even if you did the most effective DEAR MAN, sometimes the environment is so powerful that no matter how effective you are, you won't get what you want. In that case, Radical Acceptance and other Distress Tolerance skills (Chapter 2) can be helpful to cope with the situation.

DEAR MAN SKILL

What to say:

Describe the situation. Start off by describing the facts of the situation. What's going on that is leading you to make your request or say no? Avoid expressing opinions or feelings at this point.

> Example 1: Hi, Amanda! You know how the other day I was out sick?
>
> Example 2: Mom, I know you said you want me to clean my room, and I have that huge math test tomorrow.

Express your feelings. How is the situation making you feel? Focus on yourself using "I feel" statements.

> Example 1: I'm feeling stressed because I missed some really important material in math and social studies that day.
>
> Example 2: I'm feeling really stressed about it, as math is my toughest subject.

Assert what you want or say no explicitly. Be clear and specific in what you want.

> Example 1: I was wondering if I could borrow your notes from that day?
>
> Example 2: I know I probably should have cleaned my room earlier since I knew this test was coming, and I didn't. Today is really not a good time for me to do it.

Reinforce the person ahead of time for granting your request/accepting your rejection. Before you DEAR MAN someone, think about what's in it for the other person to give you what you want, and make

(Adapted from Linehan, 2015; Rathus and Miller, 2015)

that clear when you ask or say "no." The reward could be something tangible (such as "I'll do the same for you when you are in this situation," "I'll do my chores/homework before I go out," an offer to do something else for them, etc.) or intangible (such as "It'd mean a lot to me," or "I'd really appreciate it," or otherwise expressing appreciation). Reinforcement will increase the likelihood of success.

> Example 1: You always take such great notes, and I would really appreciate your help. Of course, if you are ever out sick, you are welcome to borrow my notes, too!

> Example 2: Can I please just do it tomorrow, and in the future, I'll be more mindful about cleaning my room in advance if I know I have a test coming up? I know it's just as important to you as it is to me to do well in this class. I would really appreciate your understanding.

How to say it:

Be **M**indful. Stay focused on your goal. Ignore distractions and changes of topic by the other person. Be prepared to repeat your request or your "no" while remaining calm.

> Example 1: In response to the other person's concern that the notes won't be good enough: "Oh, something is better than nothing, and I trust you that you take good enough notes. I would really appreciate it!"

> Example 2: In response to your parent's response that your room needs to be cleaned up today: "I know I should have done it before, and I just can't do it now because I really need to study so I can do well."

Appear confident. Even if you don't feel confident in your communication, look as if you are! Make eye contact, stand up straight, and use a confident voice. Don't mumble, whisper, or give up.

Negotiate. If the person responds no, be willing to give in order to get. What are you willing to do to meet your needs? Are you willing to reduce what you are asking for even a little bit? Are you willing to do a little bit of what the person is asking for instead of saying no completely? Offer alternative solutions. If you become stuck, ask for the other person's input (such as "What can we do about this?").

> Example 1: In response to the other person being hesitant to give you her notes, you might say: "Well, instead of taking them home to copy, can we go to the school office and make copies there? Or can I just take pictures of your notes on my phone?"

> Example 2: If your parent insists on your room being cleaned today, you might say: "I'll stack all the clothes on my chair so my room looks cleaner and then go through them tomorrow when I get home from school," or "I really think doing it today will lead me to get a lower grade on the test. What do you suggest we do?" Or "How about I not only clean my room after the test, but I also load the dishwasher tomorrow after dinner?"

MAINTAIN RELATIONSHIPS WITH GIVE

WHAT YOU'LL NEED

- The person with whom you need to talk
- A piece of paper or your DBT journal
- A pen or pencil
- A comfortable space where you won't be disturbed

GIVE skills are helpful tools to build and maintain positive relationships with others. These skills can be used when talking and/or listening to someone. They don't need to be used in any particular order.

BE **G**ENTLE: Be respectful and nice. Use a gentle tone of voice. Refrain from "giving attitude." If you need to express anger, use your words.

ACT **I**NTERESTED: Make eye contact, and use nonverbal and verbal communication to show interest. Don't interrupt or talk over the person, make faces, or multitask. Be patient and sensitive if the person asks to have the conversation at another time.

VALIDATE: Communicate that you understand where the other person is coming from and that you believe that the person's thoughts, feelings, or actions make sense in some way (even if you don't agree). Ask any questions with curiosity rather than judgment. Here are some suggestions:

(Adapted from Linehan, 2015; Rathus and Miller, 2015)

- "So, you are saying [summarize what they are saying]. Have I got that right?"
- "It's understandable that you think/feel that or behaved that way because . . ."
- "Anyone would think/feel/do that!"
- "I realize this may be hard to hear."

It's also validating to act based on what they are saying.

Examples: Give a hug, pass a tissue, help problem-solve if the person wants your help.

USE AN **E**ASY MANNER: Smile and joke if appropriate. Relax your body, and use more approachable body language.

INSTRUCTIONS

1. Approach someone or allow yourself to be approached by someone with whom you can have a conversation. It can be an everyday conversation or something serious.

2. Think about your priorities in this situation. In any interpersonal situation, you can have one of three priorities:

   a. Obtaining your objective: getting what you want/saying no to something you don't want to do

   b. Building or maintaining a relationship

   c. Maintaining your self-respect

   If your #1 priority is building or maintaining the relationship, proceed with the next steps. If obtaining your objective is important, too, you will want to weave in these skills with the DEAR MAN skills (see page 94).

3. Use GIVE skills in talking to and listening to the other person.

4. Come back and write about your experience. What was the result of using GIVE skills?

TAKEAWAYS

How did it feel to use GIVE skills? How do you think the other person felt? Hopefully, practicing this skill gave you some ideas for what you can do to build and maintain relationships with others. GIVE skills can be particularly helpful with difficult and emotional topics, as these strategies can help keep you calm to maintain your effectiveness, lighten the tone of the conversation, increase your self-esteem when you feel mastery about how you handled a challenging situation, and of course enhance the relationship.

FOSTER SELF-RESPECT WITH FAST

> ## WHAT YOU'LL NEED
>
> - The person with whom you need to talk
> - A piece of paper or your DBT journal
> - A pen or pencil
> - A comfortable space where you won't be disturbed

Can you think of a time when you were with someone who said something disrespectful, invalidating, or even racist to you or others? Have there been times when you felt guilty about how you handled a situation either by being too aggressive or too passive? Have you lied to avoid getting into trouble but then the lie backfired? FAST skills will help you feel good about yourself when engaging with other people.

BE **F**AIR: Be fair in your attempt to get what you want. Validate yourself and the other person's perspective. Don't sacrifice yourself to make other people happy or sacrifice others to get what you want.

(NO) **A**POLOGIES: Don't overapologize for sticking up for yourself, being you, asking for something, or acting according to your values. Apologies imply that you are wrong; apologizing all the time can reduce self-esteem. Conversely, if you wronged someone, don't underapologize; acknowledge your mistake.

S TICK TO YOUR VALUES AND BELIEFS: Don't betray your values to get what you want, get someone to like you, fit in, or avoid saying no to someone.

BE **T** RUTHFUL: Be honest. Avoid lying, acting helpless when you aren't, creating excuses, or exaggerating. A pattern of lying erodes our self-respect over time.

INSTRUCTIONS

1. You can practice this exercise in two ways:
   a. Write down a situation where someone disrespected or invalidated you or others, and you want to follow up with them about it OR
   b. Approach someone with whom you can have a conversation
2. Think about your priorities in this situation. In any interpersonal situation, you can have one of three priorities:
   a. Obtaining your objective: getting what you want/saying no to something you don't want to do
   b. Building or maintaining a relationship
   c. Maintaining your self-respect

   If your #1 priority is maintaining your self-respect, proceed with the next step. If obtaining your objective and/or maintaining the relationship is important, too, you will want to weave in these skills with the DEAR MAN and/or GIVE skills (see pages 97-98).

(Adapted from Linehan, 2015; Rathus and Miller, 2015)

3. If you are planning in advance how to use these skills, write down how you will use the FAST skills. Otherwise, practice them while talking to and listening to another person.

4. If you're planning what to say in advance, practice using your FAST skills so they feel comfortable. If you're going to email/text your FAST script to someone, finalize it. Then, go and do it!

5. Come back and write about your experience. What was the result of using FAST skills?

TAKEAWAYS

Standing up for ourselves and using FAST skills may be the hardest interpersonal effectiveness skill because there is a risk of angering or disappointing someone. Yet, the impact on your self-worth and self-esteem is huge! Remember, no one can take away your self-respect unless you give it up! Prioritizing self-respect and values is not selfish. Balancing what you want and need and what another person wants and needs might be a middle path for self-respect. Moreover, effectively using GIVE skills with others improves relationships, which also enhances self-respect.

REDUCE CONFLICT BY THINKING ABOUT IT DIFFERENTLY
Giving the benefit of the doubt

WHAT YOU'LL NEED

- The person with whom you need to talk
- A piece of paper or your DBT journal
- A pen or pencil
- A comfortable space where you won't be disturbed

Can you think of times when you assumed the worst about people's intentions or behavior? You might have thought they didn't care about you, were ignoring you, or were inconsiderate or selfish. It must have been painful for you to feel that way! Your assumptions about their behaviors likely influenced your choices and behaviors and perhaps created conflict and more distance in the relationships (and more stress in your life). To stop that cycle, Dr. Rathus and Dr. Miller developed the THINK skills. We might be right *or* wrong in our interpretations. If we give people the benefit of the doubt, we can approach them in a calmer emotional state, allowing us to communicate more productively, hear them out, and cope with what happened more effectively.

T H I N K : Stop and consider that the other person might have another viewpoint.

H AVE EMPATHY: Can you feel for the other person? Put yourself in their shoes.

I NTERPRETATIONS: List three to five possible explanations for the other person's behavior. At least one explanation should mean no harm was intended.

N OTICE: Write down ways that the other person shows they care, help, or are trying to improve things. Or, write down ways the other person may be struggling with their own stressors, which could be interfering with interpersonal effectiveness.

USE **K** INDNESS: Using DEAR MAN, GIVE, and FAST skills, write a script of what you will say to this person. Use kindness and curiosity in your approach, keeping your THINK skills in mind.

INSTRUCTIONS

1. Identify someone with whom you want to reduce conflict and anger and make peace.

2. Write about the situation that caused the conflict with the person, including your interpretations about the other person.

3. Use THINK skills to help think about the situation differently.

4. Go and talk to the person about the conflict, keeping your THINK skills in mind.

5. Come back and write about your experience. What was the result of using THINK skills?

(Adapted from Rathus and Miller, 2015)

TAKEAWAYS

Were you successful in generating reasonable possible explanations for the person's behavior? How did it feel to give the person the benefit of the doubt and approach them about the situation with curiosity rather than anger? Did you feel more mastery and control of yourself and the situation? How did/would you feel if your interpretations were correct, but you still handled the situation using Interpersonal Effectiveness skills?

If you struggled with this skill, remember that the THINK skill is most helpful after you've decreased the intensity of the emotion somewhat or have given yourself some time before you react. By continuing to practice this skill, you will likely have less conflict in your life and therefore less worry and stress!

MINDFULNESS OF OTHERS
Being present in your relationships

> **WHAT YOU'LL NEED**
> - Another person

It's easy to get caught up in the whirlwind of our lives and lose track of the people we care about. Even if we're with them, we might be multitasking or thinking about other things. It can feel frustrating to be worried and anxious about stuff and then have people get mad or hurt by our inattentiveness! At the same time, relationships need attention, or they wither and die. Mindfulness of Others helps us be present in our relationships so they can be maintained and flourish. This can also help reduce overall stress! There is some overlap between this skill and the GIVE and THINK skills. If those skills are more helpful, use those! Mindfulness of Others is just another way of thinking about similar strategies.

INSTRUCTIONS

1. Approach someone or allow yourself to be approached by someone you care about.
2. Choose a mindfulness practice from the following three options. Feel free to rotate among the options as well. All three have their benefits!

Option #1: Observe the other person and your interaction with that person:

1. Pay attention to the other person with interest and curiosity.

2. Focus solely on the other person; don't multitask!

3. Let go of focusing on yourself. Don't talk only about yourself or get caught up in what you are feeling or will say next in response. Pay attention to what the other person is saying and doing. This is particularly helpful with anxiety, in reducing our concerns about how *we* are doing and what the other person thinks of us.

4. Notice your judgments about the person, and let them go.

5. Give up needing to be right. It's validating to the other person to honor their perspective even if you don't agree.

Option #2: Describe the other person and your interaction with that person:

1. Replace judgments with facts. What's actually going on? What is the person saying, doing, and expressing?

2. Let go of assumptions and interpretations you're making about what the other person is thinking about you. You can't know unless you ask!

3. Avoid questioning the person's intentions (unless you have a good reason to do so). Just because the person's words or actions had a certain effect does not mean that was the person's intention.

4. Use your THINK skills, and give the benefit of the doubt.

(Adapted from Linehan, 2015)

Option #3: Participate fully in the relationship:

1. Throw yourself entirely into the interaction, going with the flow instead of trying to control it.

2. Let go of self-consciousness and saying/doing the right/wrong thing.

TAKEAWAYS

How did it feel to be mindful with someone else? Was it a nice reprieve from the stresses of your life to attend to someone you care about? Did your mind wander to your stresses? If so, could you bring your attention back? If so, you were practicing Mindfulness of Others! If you practice this regularly, your life might become a little less stressful because at least your relationships (or some of them) are on solid ground.

WHERE YOU HOPE
TO BE SOON

Now that you've learned how to improve your interpersonal effectiveness, take some time to journal how you could use the Interpersonal Effectiveness skills in this chapter to assert yourself more effectively, build and maintain meaningful relationships and reduce conflict, and foster self-respect. Think about your goals and the people in your life: family members, friends, romantic partners, coworkers, or people you'd like to get to know better. Write down one to three specific ways you could use the DEAR MAN, GIVE, FAST, THINK, and Mindfulness of Others strategies to improve your daily life. The more you practice these skills, the easier they will come naturally to you. As a result, you'll feel more contented and in control of your life.

Chapter Five

WALKING THE MIDDLE PATH

When we feel stressed and anxious, our perspective can become narrow and our emotions can intensify. To help us take a more flexible approach to life experiences, Drs. Linehan, Rathus, and Miller developed a fifth DBT module of skills called Walking the Middle Path. Walking the Middle Path skills help us take a more flexible approach to life experiences. Walking the middle path doesn't mean a 50/50 compromise. Rather, it means considering *all* the facts—past circumstances, the present situation, and future possibilities and consequences—and synthesizing that information to help you be as effective as possible in achieving your relationship goals. If you, your family, or close friends argue frequently, these skills might be helpful to share with them, as well.

THE MIDDLE PATH SKILLS IN ACTION

Hanna was stressed because she believed her partner, Kira, wasn't paying enough attention to her. As a result, Hanna fluctuated between withdrawing from and ignoring Kira and starting arguments about the lack of time spent together. Walking the Middle Path skills helped Hanna talk to Kira about how she felt and hear Kira's perspective about the situation. By talking and understanding each other's perspectives, the couple came up with a plan that satisfied both of their needs. They also agreed to keep talking about these issues rather than keeping their concerns bottled inside or exploding at each other.

Noah was struggling in school, and his parents were on his back about his grades and assignments. Sometimes he ignored them when they attempted to talk to him; other times, screaming arguments erupted. Noah felt anger about the unfairness of the situation, thinking, *I just don't care about school or my future*, and shame that he was in this position. These extremes in his behaviors, thoughts, and emotions got in the way of his productivity. Walking the middle path helped Noah recognize the circumstances that led to this situation and validated his and his parents' perspectives. He could then approach his parents in a calm way about what they could do to be helpful.

These examples illustrate the challenges of responding to life circumstances in the extreme. Intense ineffective emotions, polarized thinking, and impulsive behaviors may feel satisfying in the moment, but they take us further from our goals. Walking the Middle Path skills can free you from these cycles of emotional and interpersonal chaos and guide you toward living a balanced and harmonious life.

WHERE YOU ARE NOW

Take a few minutes to write about the obstacles that get in the way of feeling positive about yourself and enjoying healthy relationships with others.

- Do you set yourself up for failure because you aren't recognizing the obstacles that are making life more challenging for you?

- Are you passive about the challenges in your life because you have given up trying to change anything?

- Are changes and transitions challenging for you?

- Do you tend to blame yourself as the sole cause of all your problems, or do you blame everyone else?

- When you disagree with someone, can you see their perspective even if you don't agree with it, or do you get stuck in "I'm right; they're wrong"?

- Do people have a hard time understanding your perspective? When they don't see your perspective or understand you, do you find that it is hard to emotionally recover and maybe even start telling yourself that you are wrong?

- Do you ever reward yourself or others for doing what you want, or do you focus on what you or someone else did that was "bad" and use punishment as a response?

THINKING AND ACTING DIALECTICALLY

> ## WHAT YOU'LL NEED
> - A piece of paper or your DBT journal
> - A pen or pencil

Do you tend to get stuck in thinking traps like all-or-nothing thinking, catastrophizing, disqualifying positives and focusing only on the negatives, assuming you know what someone is thinking and feeling, believing that you/someone else/a situation "should" be a certain way, generalizing from specific situations, or blaming yourself for things over which you have no control? As a result, do you make choices that cause problems for you? Thinking and acting dialectically is a helpful way to climb out of these traps. Let's learn about this. According to DBT, dialectics teaches us that:

- Two seemingly opposite truths can both be true at the same time, and we can look for the kernel of truth in both sides to come to greater understanding and less extreme thinking, feeling, and behaving. For example, instead of believing "I'm doing the best I can" *or* "I should be doing more," dialectics teaches us that "I'm doing the best I can *and* I need to do more to achieve my goals."
- We are all connected to each other in some way. What we do affects others, and what others do affects us.

- Change is the only constant. Nothing lasts forever. Each moment is a new and different moment.

Dialectics is a helpful way to think and act more flexibly and get "unstuck" when in conflict with yourself, others, and the world. Read on to learn how to put this into practice.

INSTRUCTIONS

1. Describe a situation where you did not think or act dialectically; where you got stuck in thinking traps described above and responded accordingly.

2. Identify which of the following suggestions could have been more effective in your situation, and describe how you could have used them to be more dialectical:

   a. Use "both/and" wording instead of "either/or" or "but"; avoid extreme words such as "always," "never," and instead use "sometimes" or just describe the situation.

   b. Ask yourself, *What am I missing? What is being left out?* Dig deep to find the kernel of truth in every side of the situation. If you are in conflict with someone, try to see things from their perspective.

   c. Open up to alternatives. Nothing is absolutely true/untrue, right/wrong, or good/bad.

   d. Express how you feel, and be open to what other people have to say. Say "I feel [insert emotion] when you say/do [insert descriptive behavior]" instead of blaming the other person with statements like "You are . . ." or "You should . . ."

(Adapted from Linehan, 2015; Rathus and Miller, 2015)

e. Agree to disagree at times, accepting that differing opinions can be valid, even if you don't agree.

f. Ask what someone meant by what they said or did instead of assuming their intentions or meaning.

g. Remember: we're all connected. Treat others as you want to be treated, and focus on similarities, not differences.

h. Allow for change and embrace it. If change is hard for you, practice getting used to change with smaller things, such as taking a different route, sitting in a different chair, or changing one thing in your routine.

i. Notice your effect on others and their effects on you.

3. Describe what you think the outcome would have been if you used these strategies.

TAKEAWAYS

Were you able to move away from extremes, taking more of a middle path, integrating all the information (not just your information), becoming more effective in the situation? The more you practice, the easier it gets. Adopting a dialectical perspective can help reduce your anxiety, stress, and conflict with others and bring you more happiness, improved relationships, and greater self-confidence in your abilities.

VALIDATING OTHERS

WHAT YOU'LL NEED

- Another person

Validation means communicating that what someone is thinking, feeling, or doing makes sense and is understandable in some way. It requires putting ourselves in the other person's shoes and seeing the world from their perspective. When we validate others, it creates powerful and positive changes in feelings and relationships by decreasing intense emotions and reducing conflict. When you show an openness to someone's perspective and see their kernel of truth, they'll be more responsive to what you have to say. Validation gets tricky for two reasons:

1. People might think that validation means that they are agreeing with the other person, which is not accurate. You can understand why someone might be thinking, feeling, or doing something even if you don't agree with it.

2. It can be hard to find something to validate when the whole situation seems problematic. One way around this is to validate the emotion that someone is feeling. Let's say your friend is complaining that they are doing poorly in school when they've been skipping classes. You don't want to validate the lack of effort, but you can validate how disappointing or frustrating it is to not do well in school.

INSTRUCTIONS

Practice the following validation skills the next time you have a conversation with someone who is feeling upset about something.

NOTE: These suggested ways of validating are organized from easiest/least impactful to hardest/most impactful.

1. Pay attention and actively listen—avoid multitasking.

2. Summarize what the person is saying without judgment. Repeat what you heard or observed to make sure you are on the same page. Be open to being corrected if you are wrong.

3. "Mind read" (if you know them well) or ask questions. Pay attention to what the person may be communicating through body language and what you know about the situation and the person. Communicate understanding through your words and/or actions. Ask questions in a curious way to determine if there is more going on than the person is telling you.

    Examples: When your friend is angry about a job interview that didn't go well because the interviewer "was a jerk," saying, "I wonder if you are also really disappointed because I know how hard you've been looking for a job?"; asking for more details with questions like "And then what happened?"

4. Express that someone's thoughts, feelings, and/or behaviors make sense based on the person's history or biology by describing *how* they do. These things could make sense even if you don't approve of them in the current context.

    Example: "It's understandable/it makes sense that you think/feel/did that because [give specific history] . . ."

(Adapted from Linehan, 2015; Rathus and Miller, 2015)

5. Normalize the person's thoughts, feelings, or behaviors based on the current context and facts. If someone's thoughts, feelings, or behaviors make sense, say so!

    Examples: "It makes sense that you feel that way!" "I did/would do the same thing!"

6. Treat the other person as an equal and capable, not as incompetent or fragile. Show that you take them seriously. Ask what they need of you, whether to just listen or to help solve their problem. Admit times when you've made mistakes.

TAKEAWAYS

Hopefully, your experience of validating someone else helped you feel effective and masterful, compassionate and accepting, and helped the other person feel understood. If it didn't go as well as you would have liked, here are some considerations for next time:

1. Sometimes we need to validate a lot to help someone reduce the intensity of their emotions or be ready to hear another perspective. It can be helpful to ask, *"Do you want to hear what I have to say, or are you not there yet? Either way is okay with me."*

2. Sometimes people repeat "That makes sense" or "I understand." Then people don't feel like the validation is genuine. Dig deep to understand the other person's perspective, and validate them thoughtfully.

3. It can be helpful to ask, *"Do you want my help, or do you want me to just listen?"* Sometimes, people need someone just to hear them out before they are open to problem-solving with them, and sometimes they just want to vent.

COPING WITH INVALIDATION AND VALIDATING OURSELVES

WHAT YOU'LL NEED

- A piece of paper or your DBT journal
- A pen or pencil

Invalidation refers to communication that implies that your thoughts, feelings, and/or actions don't make sense, are "stupid" or "wrong," are an overreaction, or are something you should "just get over." It can occur when someone ignores you, doesn't "get" you, denies important facts in your life, treats you unequally, or mistreats you. These forms of invalidation can be incredibly painful. If only the whole world was skilled in validating other people! However, that's not the case, so it's important to learn how to cope effectively when we do experience invalidation and how to validate ourselves if we can't get that from our environment.

First, it's important to be mindful of what *we* might be doing that may lead others to invalidate us:

- Do you struggle with stating your needs and wants directly?
- Do you have a hard time saying no?
- Do you tend to keep your thoughts and emotions to yourself, so it's hard for others to know what you are experiencing?

- Do you invalidate others (intentionally or not), including jumping into problem-solving or sharing your opinion without being asked?
- Are you staying in an invalidating relationship?
- Do you engage in self-criticism, self-judgment, and self-invalidation in the presence of others?
- Do you struggle with responding effectively in challenging situations?

If you answered yes to any of these questions, it may be helpful to think about how you can use the skills in this chapter and book to help you change these behaviors so you are less likely to receive invalidation from others. Invalidation happens to everyone, so keep reading to learn how to cope with invalidation when it occurs.

INSTRUCTIONS

1. Write down a description of an invalidating situation. Identify the painful thoughts and emotions you are experiencing.

2. Check the Facts (page 71) to determine whether your response to the situation fits the facts.

3. If your response does fit the facts, choose any of the following strategies that could be helpful for you, and write down what you can say or do to implement them in this circumstance:

   a. Validate yourself the way you would validate others (page 116). Acknowledge that your reaction makes sense. Remind yourself that just because someone else doesn't see the validity in the situation doesn't mean the situation isn't valid.

b.   Describe and let go of any judgments you have about your valid thoughts, feelings, and/or behaviors. Describe and let go of other people's judgments that they have about you and your response. Remember, judgments are judgments, not facts.

c.   Get help and support. Reach out to others who can provide you with validation. This is super helpful in moving forward from invalidation.

d.   Use Radical Acceptance (page 51) to help accept the person who invalidated you. This can be hard and takes time.

e.   Use FAST skills (page 100) to stick up for yourself to the invalidating person.

4. If your response *does not* fit the facts and you overreacted, misinterpreted, or were ineffective (which can happen sometimes!):

a.   Accept that your reaction did not fit the facts and didn't make sense. This can be hard to admit (and you can self-validate the pain of being invalidated, even if the other person is right).

b.   Change the ineffective thoughts, feelings, and/or behaviors so you don't get invalidated again.

c.   Act Opposite (page 77) to feelings of guilt about engaging in the invalid response. Apologize if you went against your values, and repair what's been broken in the relationship. Commit to not engaging in the behavior again.

d.   Describe and let go of the judgments you have about yourself or others. Judging and blaming yourself or others just makes the situation worse.

(Adapted from Linehan, 2015; Rathus and Miller, 2015)

e.   Practice being dialectical and self-validating by reminding yourself that all behaviors are caused by behaviors that happened previously. You responded the way you did based on your previous behaviors and responses and those of others. We all make mistakes.

f.   Use Distress Tolerance skills, especially Self-Soothing (page 39), to help cope with invalidation. Even if you were in the wrong, invalidation is still painful.

TAKEAWAYS

Invalidation can be incredibly hurtful. Hopefully, these strategies can help you cope more effectively. Coping with invalidation also requires skills discussed in earlier chapters of this book. If you practice these strategies, they'll help you be more effective in these situations and in your choices that come from these experiences.

BEHAVIORAL STRATEGIES TO INCREASE THE BEHAVIORS WE WANT IN OURSELVES AND OTHERS

WHAT YOU'LL NEED

- A piece of paper or your DBT journal
- A pen or pencil

Are there certain habits or behaviors you wish you did regularly? Maybe completing schoolwork immediately instead of waiting until the last minute; practicing a musical instrument, sport, or craft; or completing a chore on your own without needing to be reminded? Telling ourselves to "just do it" is often not enough to make it happen. Punishing ourselves by shaming ourselves when we don't do our desired behaviors doesn't work either—it just makes us feel worse.

Now, are there certain habits or behaviors that you wished *others* did regularly, like talking nicely to you, cleaning up after themselves, or doing nice things for you? If we keep our preferences to ourselves or nag, criticize, or demand, we're unlikely to get the desired response, and it may sour our relationship.

In either case, if we want a behavior to occur *more*, we need to identify what that behavior is and *reinforce* it when it occurs. Reinforcement refers to any consequence of a behavior that increases the likelihood of that behavior occurring again. There are two types of reinforcement:

1. Positive Reinforcement increases a behavior with rewards. *Examples of Reinforcement for Yourself: desired grades, money, presents, desired attention, compliments and praise, intrinsic satisfaction, or a mental "yay me". Examples of Reinforcement for Others: compliments and praise, doing something nice for them or something they want you to do, suggesting fun activities they would enjoy.*

2. Negative Reinforcement increases a behavior with relief from something aversive or unpleasant. *Examples: Using your DBT skills to cope with negative and ineffective emotions, taking medication to alleviate physical pain, completing a chore that a parent keeps reminding you to do, completing late assignments to remove an incomplete grade.*

Sometimes, a desired behavior requires multiple steps to achieve it. Shaping a behavior refers to reinforcing the small steps that are necessary to achieve the larger goal. For example, if you have a large research paper to write, you might reward yourself when you choose the topic, then again after doing the research, writing the outline, completing each paragraph or section, and finally submitting the paper. If you wait to reinforce yourself only for submitting the paper, it might not be enough to get you through all the steps it takes to get there.

For reinforcement of a behavior to work:

- The reinforcement needs to occur *immediately* after the behavior you want to reinforce.
- The reinforcement needs to be reinforcing to the person (if you are reinforcing someone with chocolate and they don't like chocolate, the reinforcement won't work).
- Don't surround the reinforcement with criticism (if you complete an assignment early, don't beat yourself up for not *always* doing so).

INSTRUCTIONS

1. Write down a specific behavior that you want to do or you want someone else to do. Be as behaviorally specific as possible; how would you know you've achieved that desired behavior?
2. Identify a reinforcer for that behavior. (If you have a hard time identifying a reinforcer, try using an activity you do already; for example, you can't text with your friends until you complete your homework for the day or you can watch a TV show after working on your essay for 50 minutes.)
3. Now, whenever the behavior (or the small step toward a larger goal) occurs, reinforce immediately.
4. Write down the outcome of reinforcing a desired behavior. What did you observe when you used Reinforcement?

(Adapted from Linehan, 2015; Rathus and Miller, 2015)

TAKEAWAYS

So often we focus on what we or others are doing "wrong." What was it like to focus on what you or others were doing well? Hopefully, the experience of reinforcing was positive, and the desired outcome was achieved, too. If it did work, challenge yourself further by identifying how you can use this skill to target other desired behaviors!

BEHAVIORAL STRATEGIES TO REDUCE BEHAVIORS WE DON'T WANT IN OURSELVES AND OTHERS

WHAT YOU'LL NEED

- A piece of paper or your DBT journal
- A pen or pencil

Are there certain behaviors that you wish you or others didn't do? In these situations, the most effective strategy is to identify what behaviors you *want* to do or want others to do and reinforce those effective behaviors, as we discussed in the previous exercise. There might also be times when it could be useful to pair reinforcement of desired behaviors with strategies to decrease or stop unwanted behaviors such as:

EXTINCTION ("ACTIVE IGNORING") decreases a behavior by stopping previously provided reinforcement. For instance, let's say you have urges to use an ineffective behavior. If you stop acting on the urges, the urges will decrease via extinction. Let's say you have a younger sibling who makes annoying sounds outside your bedroom door because they want to be with you. You keep yelling at them to stop. Yelling at your sibling actually reinforces their behavior because they get your attention, even if it's negative attention. If you want your sibling's behavior to stop, extinction teaches us to ignore the behavior. Don't respond or say anything at all! If you use extinction, keep ignoring when urges or behaviors increase, and be consistent. It may be helpful to give them a heads-up that you are doing this, and make sure to reinforce desired behaviors.

SATIATION provides a reinforcer before it's necessary. For example, if a problematic behavior helps you feel better or results in validation, satiation teaches us that if we meet that function some other way, the urge won't come up. If your sibling wants to be with you, satiation teaches us that if you schedule other times to hang out with your sibling, they won't engage in annoying behaviors to get your attention. Satiation is a way to avoid needing to extinguish or ignore problematic behaviors by avoiding the issue in the first place!

PUNISHMENT is a consequence after a behavior that suppresses that behavior. We often use punishment on ourselves, beating ourselves up for doing something we "shouldn't" have done, and people often use punishment on others, such as yelling, criticizing, adding chores or extra assignments, removing privileges, and so on. However, the problem with punishment is that it doesn't teach people what *to do*! It's more effective to reinforce desired behavior than to punish undesired behavior; focus on the positives instead of the negatives.

INSTRUCTIONS

1. Write down a behavior in which you or someone else engages that you want to stop. Be as specific as possible.

2. Write down what extinction or active ignoring would look like to decrease or stop this behavior.

3. What behavior do you want to reinforce instead? How could you do that? Could satiation work, too? If so, how?

4. Put your ideas into practice and then write down the outcome. How did it go?

TAKEAWAYS

Decreasing behaviors is hard to do, especially when they're reinforcing in some way. The keys with using these strategies are time and consistency. Most importantly, it's absolutely necessary to reinforce desired behaviors. Keep practicing!

(Adapted from Linehan, 2015; Rathus and Miller, 2015)

WHERE YOU HOPE
TO BE SOON

Now that you've learned some strategies to walk the middle path, take some time to journal how using Dialectics (page 113), Validation (page 116), coping with Invalidation (page 120), and behavioral strategies to increase desired behaviors (page 124) and decrease undesired behaviors (page 128) could be helpful to you. Envision a future where you respond to life's challenges in a more flexible and balanced way. What would walking the middle path with wisdom and ease look like for you? Write down one to three things that you can do to strengthen your ability to walk the middle path in your daily life.

- How can you be more dialectical?

- How can you be more validating to yourself and others?

- How can you use behavioral strategies to increase desired behaviors and decrease undesired behaviors in yourself and others?

Remember, the more you practice these skills, the more naturally they will come to you.

PART TWO

PUTTING IT TOGETHER

Chapters 1 through 5 provided examples of how different skills are helpful in managing anxiety. Sometimes, we need to use skills from multiple areas to cope effectively with stressful situations. Now that you've learned about and practiced the different DBT skills, the following chapters will help you further implement them in your daily lives.

Chapter Six

HOW TO DEAL WITH ANXIETY-INDUCING SCENARIOS

There are stressful situations we can anticipate and ones that surprise us! This chapter provides suggestions for various DBT skills you can use to respond skillfully to common teen stressors. These are suggestions not rules; feel free to tailor them to your needs.

WHEN APPROACHING TOUGH SITUATIONS

Some stressors are time-limited (like taking a test), and others continue for an indeterminate amount of time (like dealing with a strained relationship or a chronic health condition). You can effectively handle *all* these circumstances with DBT skills.

The +1 Rule: How many skills should I use?
When dealing with stressful situations, the "+1 Rule," based on the work of DBT expert Dr. Julie Brown, is helpful for identifying the number of DBT skills you should use to get through a difficult situation. To use this:

1. Rate your current distress on a scale of 0 to 5 (0 feeling no distress; 5 feeling most distressed).

2. Add 1 to that number (hence, the +1 Rule).

3. The total number is the number of skills you need to cope with that situation! For example:

   a. If you are feeling no distress (0 + 1 = 1), you should still be using at least one skill to help maintain the peace, such as Mindfulness (Chapter 1), ABC PLEASE skills (page 56), Interpersonal Effectiveness skills (Chapter 4), and Walking the Middle Path skills (page 110).

   b. If you are feeling the most distressed (5 + 1 = 6), you should plan to use six skills to get through the situation.

   c. Moderate levels of distress will require a number of skills to be effective.

The Cope-Ahead Plan for Upcoming Difficult Situations

Cope Ahead is a useful skill to help you cope effectively with anticipated stressful situations. Here are the steps:

1. Identify an upcoming situation that you anticipate will cause you emotional distress. Describe the facts of the situation. What specific emotions will the situation cause?

2. Identify the DBT skills that will help you cope effectively with this situation. Feel free to look back at previous chapters to find the right skills for you.

3. Imagine yourself in the situation using the skills you identified. What would you say, think, and do?

(Adapted from Linehan, 2015; Rathus and Miller, 2015)

4. As you rehearse the situation in your mind, identify possible obstacles that would impede your effective skill use. Troubleshoot these problems. How can you get around them? Do your best to identify the obstacles based on past experiences in similar situations or obstacles that are your greatest fears.

5. Participate in the actual situation, and implement your Cope-Ahead plan if needed.

6. Learn from your experience. Did you need your Cope-Ahead plan? If so, did it go smoothly? If it did, reinforce yourself for adequately preparing and implementing these skills! If you ran into unexpected obstacles, identify them and write down what you can do differently next time.

Next, we'll explore different scenarios with plans to help you put all the DBT skills together. You'll need to personalize these plans to your specific situation. If your stressor isn't listed here, check out the "Skills in Action" sections in previous chapters that also provide suggestions for how to use DBT skills in particular circumstances.

Preparing for an Exam

You have an important exam coming up. This class is your toughest subject, and you've done poorly on past exams. You have a lot going on and no time to study. You're stressed!

DBT TOOL KIT

- Use TIPP (page 47) to calm your body right now.
- Practice Radical Acceptance (page 51) to accept what you can and cannot change about this situation.
- Problem-Solve (page 74) how to get your studying done. Include Positive Reinforcement (page 125) to keep yourself motivated.
- Use Opposite Action (page 77) when feeling anxious and tempted to avoid studying.
- Participate mindfully (page 19) in your work. Use Mindfulness of Thoughts (page 25) or Emotions (page 59) if they are distracting you. Encouragement (page 42) and Self-Validation (page 120) can also keep you motivated and doing the best you can.
- Use PLEASE skills (page 56) to care for your physical well-being even if you don't think you have time. You need your strength!

Test/Performance Anxiety

You studied for a test, but you've panicked during the test before such that your mind goes blank and you can't focus. You want to prevent this from happening again.

DBT TOOL KIT

- Before your test, use Cope Ahead (page 135) to help you identify what you are most afraid of in the situation. Imagine yourself participating in the situation effectively. Rehearse this every day leading up to the test. If you can imagine yourself being successful, you're more likely to be!

- Use TIPP (page 47) to calm your body when you are becoming physically anxious before and during the test.

- Use Opposite Action (page 77) if you feel stuck during the test. Instead of shutting down, find a question you can answer. You can always go back to the harder questions once you've gotten the easier ones out of the way.

- Use Mindfulness of Activities (page 19) to fully participate in the test.

- Use Mindfulness of Thoughts (page 25) to observe and let go of any negative thoughts or judgments that get in the way of focusing.

- Use Encouragement (page 42) and Self-Validation (page 120) to remain motivated and feeling compassionate toward yourself.

Attending a Social Event

You need to attend a social event that is outside of your comfort zone. You feel very nervous about embarrassing yourself or being alone among others.

DBT TOOL KIT

- Before the event, Cope Ahead (page 135) to help identify what you are most afraid of in the situation. Imagine yourself effectively participating in the situation using the skills below. Rehearse as often as possible. If you can imagine yourself being successful, you are more likely to be!

- Use Opposite Action (page 77) to act opposite to urges to avoid attending, and participate in the event all the way!

- Use Mindfulness of Thoughts (page 25) to observe and let go of any negative thoughts or judgments that come up, and then keep practicing Opposite Action.

- Use GIVE skills (page 97) and Mindfulness of Others (page 106) to build and maintain relationships with others at the event.

- Use TIPP (page 47) to reduce physical anxiety symptoms.

- Use Encouragement (page 42) and Self-Validation (page 120) to motivate and feel compassionate toward yourself.

Coping with Distressing Current Events

You hear about yet another distressing, scary, or unsettling event in the news. You're feeling depressed, anxious, and angry about current circumstances and for the future.

DBT TOOL KIT

- Use Mindfulness of Emotions (page 84) to label your emotions, allow yourself to experience your emotions, and let them come and go.

- Practice Radical Acceptance (page 51) to accept your emotions and what you can and cannot change about the circumstances.

- Distract yourself with ACCEPTS (page 36) and use Self-Soothing (page 39) to tolerate your distress.

- IMPROVE the Moment (page 41) by identifying any bright spots about the current events (such as bringing people together, spurring people to act) and taking a break by unplugging.

- If you don't want to talk about the current events anymore, use your DEAR MAN GIVE FAST (pages 91, 97, 100) to say so.

- Use Mindfulness of Gratitude (page 28) to notice the good happening in your life.

- Practice Mindfulness of Thoughts (page 25) to observe your thoughts and let them go so you don't get stuck in them.

- Practice Opposite Action (page 77). If your fear or sadness is future-oriented, focus on making the best of today. Live your best life, engage in pleasant activities, and work toward long-term goals. Channel your anger into productive action, such as getting involved in a good cause.

- Use Dialectics (page 113) to think about perspectives other than your own. You don't have to agree with the other perspectives, but greater understanding will help you be more effective.

Focusing on Schoolwork When Experiencing Difficult Family Circumstances

- -

Problems at home, such as financial stressors, physical illness or mental health concerns, high conflict between family members, or increased responsibilities, can make it hard to focus on schoolwork. You feel stressed and overwhelmed and don't know how to focus or get everything done.

DBT TOOL KIT

- Validate yourself (page 120) and your family members (page 116) on the challenges everyone is facing.
- Problem-Solve (page 74) to identify what needs to be done and how you can make it happen.
- Use your DEAR MAN GIVE FAST skills (pages 91, 97, 100) to ask for help with problem-solving.
- When you are doing your schoolwork, use Mindfulness of Activities (page 19) to help focus and cope with distractions by bringing your attention back over and over again.
- Use Positive Reinforcement (page 124) to reward yourself for getting your work done and reward others for supporting you.
- Use PLEASE skills (page 69) to care for your physical well-being during this stressful time.

Friends Don't Seem to Be Hanging Out with You as Much

You worry that your friends aren't hanging out with you as much as they used to. Sometimes you just want to end the relationship before they hurt you; and other times, you can't stop reaching out to them! You're feeling sad, confused, and worried.

DBT TOOL KIT

- Use Check the Facts (page 71) to determine whether your emotion fits the facts.

- If your emotion does fit the facts, use Problem-Solving (page 74) and DEAR MAN GIVE FAST (pages 91, 97, 100) to talk to your friends about how you feel and come up with a plan.

- Use Dialectics (page 113) if you get in stuck your own thoughts and have a hard time seeing your friends' perspectives.

- Distract with ACCEPTS (page 36), Self-Soothe (page 39), and Improve the Moment (page 41) to tolerate these emotions if they do fit the facts and you and your friends can't come up with a resolution. Self-Validate (page 120) how painful that is.

- If your emotion doesn't fit the facts, use Mindfulness of Emotions (page 84) or Opposite Action (page 77) to decrease your emotion.

- Even if your emotion didn't fit the facts, Self-Validate (page 120) how painful it is to feel the way you did.

Not Wanting to Be Caught in the Middle of an Argument

- -

Your best friends or parents are fighting with each other, and you don't want to be forced to take sides. It's hard because everyone keeps coming to you to talk about their perspective. You don't know what to do!

DBT TOOL KIT

- Self-Validate (page 120) how difficult it is to be in this position.
- Access your Wise Mind (page 30) to determine what to do. Pros and Cons (page 44) could also be helpful in making this decision.
- If you decide to speak up, Cope Ahead (page 135) for what you will say and troubleshoot potential obstacles. Use DEAR MAN GIVE FAST (pages 91, 97, 100) to help you clearly express what you want or don't want from the other person. Implement your plan.
- Make sure to Validate them (page 116). Reinforce (page 124) their acceptance of your request.
- If you decide to keep quiet, distract yourself with ACCEPTS (page 36), Self-Soothe (page 39), and IMPROVE the Moment (page 41) skills to help tolerate your distress and Radical Acceptance (page 51) to help you accept your decision.
- It can also be helpful to use Dialectics (page 113) and Validation (page 116) when talking to everyone instead of thinking you need to respond by taking sides. Maybe teach them some DBT skills to help them solve their problems on their own without you!

Wanting to Say No in the Face of Peer Pressure

- -

Someone (or even a group) wants you to do something that makes you feel uncomfortable. You're worried that if you say no, they will drop you as a friend or spread rumors about you.

DBT TOOL KIT

- Check the Facts (page 71) for the emotion(s) you are feeling, the details of the situation, and the consequences you are anticipating in order to determine how to respond.

- Access your Wise Mind (page 30) or complete a Pros and Cons (page 44) to help you decide how to respond.

- Consider the DEAR MAN interpersonal factors in making a request or saying no (page 91) to help you determine your response and how strongly to respond.

- Use DEAR MAN GIVE FAST (pages 91, 97, 100) to respond (prepared in advance, if possible).

- Cope Ahead (page 135) for different possible reactions/outcomes to your response, including Positively Reinforcing (page 125) yourself for speaking up and using Distress Tolerance skills (page 33). If you don't have time to Cope Ahead because you needed to respond immediately, use these skills anyway to remain effective.

Speaking Up When Someone Expresses Different Values

Someone expressed something about race, ethnicity, religion, socio-economic status, sexual or gender identity that goes against your values or personally insults you or a group with whom you're affiliated. You're uncertain what to say, if anything.

DBT TOOL KIT

- Validate yourself (page 120) for the emotional pain experienced as a result of what they said. Use Dialectics (page 113) to Validate the other person (page 116) as to why they might be expressing that view—hopefully, you can find something about this to validate.

- Access your Wise Mind (page 30) or work through a Pros and Cons (page 44) to help you decide whether to speak up. It might also be helpful to talk to a trusted friend or adult.

- If you choose to say something, use DEAR MAN GIVE FAST (pages 91, 97, 100) to respond (prepared in advance, if possible).

- Cope Ahead (page 135) for different possible outcomes to your response (or lack of response) to help you be effective regardless of the outcome.

Setting Limits with Bosses

Your boss wants you to work longer hours, isn't giving you enough hours according to your contract, or asks you to do something that goes against your values, moral code, or maybe even the law. You need this job, but you feel uncomfortable and don't know what to do.

DBT TOOL KIT

- Validate yourself (page 120) for being in this difficult position. Use Dialectics (page 113) or THINK (page 103) to identify and validate why your boss might be making this request of you.

- Access your Wise Mind (page 30) or complete a Pros and Cons (page 44) to help you decide how to respond. Perhaps also talk to a trusted adult.

- Consider the DEAR MAN interpersonal factors in making a request or saying no (page 91) to help you determine your response and how strongly to respond.

- Use DEAR MAN GIVE FAST (pages 91, 97, 100) to respond (prepared in advance, if possible).

- Cope Ahead (page 135) for different possible reactions/outcomes to your response to help you be effective after the fact, including Positively Reinforcing (page 125) yourself for speaking up even if it doesn't go well, and using Distress Tolerance skills (page 33).

Conflict with a Parent/Caregiver

You and your parent(s)/caregiver are in a disagreement about something. You tend to respond by either avoiding the situation but feeling resentful or by yelling at them or worse. You'd like to stop fighting with them and come to an effective resolution (ideally, one in your favor).

DBT TOOL KIT

- Practice Dialectics (page 113) to help you recognize their perspective. If you honestly don't know their perspective, use your Dialectical strategies (page 114) to ask them.

- Consider the DEAR MAN interpersonal factors in making a request (page 91) to help you determine if you have everything you need to assert yourself and how strongly to assert yourself.

- Prepare and use DEAR MAN GIVE FAST skills. Pay attention to describing all the facts, expressing your emotions, expressing your request clearly, communicating how granting your request would benefit them, and validating their responses. Think about what compromise you'd be okay with, and be willing to negotiate!

- If you can't get what you want, use Distress Tolerance skills (pages 33–35), Radical Acceptance (page 51), and Self-Validation (page 120).

Fear of Being a Burden to Others

You yearn to talk to someone about how you are feeling or ask someone for help, but you don't want to burden them.

DBT TOOL KIT

- Use Emotion Identification (page 59) and Check the Facts (page 71) to determine whether your emotions fit the facts.

- Access your Wise Mind (page 30) or complete a Pros and Cons (page 44) to help you decide how to proceed.

- If you determine that your fears of possibly being a burden fit the facts (such as if the person has already asked you not to speak to them about certain topics or they don't have the energy to help), use Problem-Solving (page 74) to help you identify someone else with whom you can speak or to change the relationship dynamics with people in your life so you can go to them without them feeling burdened.

- If you determine that your concerns don't fit the facts, use Opposite Action (page 77) and reach out to that person. Use DEAR MAN GIVE FAST (pages 91, 97, 100) to communicate effectively.

- Practice Mindfulness of Others (page 106) to maintain a healthy relationship with that person to reduce the likelihood of being "a burden."

You Want to End a Toxic Relationship

You are in a relationship that's harmful to you in some way and/or gets in the way of achieving your goals or your ability to enjoy life. You may care about this person and recognize it's not healthy for you to remain in the relationship, but you feel scared and uncertain about ending it.

DBT TOOL KIT

- Use your Wise Mind (page 30) and/or Pros and Cons (page 44) to help decide whether to end the relationship.

- Self-Validate (page 120) how difficult it is to be in this position.

- Cope Ahead (page 135) to practice ending the relationship. What will you say, if anything, using DEAR MAN GIVE FAST (pages 91, 97, 100) skills? Problem-Solve issues that could get in the way of sticking to your decision; for example, if you can't cut the person completely out of your life, how you will deal with seeing each other. Implement your Cope Ahead plan.

- Practice Opposite Action for love (page 77) to reduce loving feelings toward that person and make it easier to stay away.

- Use Positive Reinforcement (page 125) on yourself for sticking to your decision and on others for supporting yourself in your decision.

- If you are in an abusive or life-threatening situation, please reach out to a trusted adult for help.

Managing Extremely High Emotional Arousal/ Panic Attacks

You are so stressed and overwhelmed by life. You might be having a panic attack. You're consumed by the intense emotions that you are feeling. You can't process any information, solve problems, or use complex skills.

DBT TOOL KIT

- Use TIPP (page 47) to calm your body right now. You might need to use more than one of these strategies to calm your body enough to use the subsequent skills.
- The 5-4-3-2-1 mindfulness practice (page 21) can also be helpful in grounding yourself in reality.
- Use other Distress Tolerance skills (pages 33–35) to tolerate the situation without making things worse. Again, you might need to use more than one.
- Use Mindfulness of Emotions (page 84) to experience the emotion like a wave that ebbs and flows and ultimately fizzles out on its own.
- Use Problem-Solving (page 74) or Opposite Action (page 77) to address the situation that prompted the emotional overload in the first place.
- Practice ABC PLEASE (pages 56–57) to reduce the likelihood of these episodes happening in the first place.

CONCLUSION

It's normal for teens to worry about lots of different things: school, friends, family, finances, your future, your country, and the world, just to name a few. Plus, you're living in a world where adults are making important choices that impact you, and you might feel like you don't have much say or control over what happens around you.

Hopefully, you've found the DBT skills described in this book helpful for taking back control of your emotions and life choices. We can't determine what other people do, but we can choose how we respond to life's stressors. I hope you have learned not to be afraid of your emotions but rather to allow yourself to experience them, assess them, and manage them more effectively. Emotions exist for a reason; use them to your advantage!

Using DBT skills can seem challenging at times. If you continue to practice them in your life, you can have a life that is a lot easier and more enjoyable without the burden of chronic stress and anxiety weighing you down. You've already survived many times what you probably thought were the hardest moments of your life! I have no doubt that with DBT in your back pocket, you will continue surviving the tough moments and flourish in a future of your creation.

APPENDIX

YOUR DBT TOOL BOX

Appendix Contents

WORKSHEETS

You've learned a lot of skills! This appendix provides handouts, charts, and templates that can help you access or create your own DBT skills cheat sheets. This way, when you're experiencing overwhelming stress and anxiety and you can't go through the entire book to refresh your memory of what to do, you have easily accessible tools to help you!

STOP IN A CRISIS

(Adapted from Linehan, 2015)

When confronted with any challenging situation in which you are uncertain how to respond, use the STOP skill. The STOP skill is super helpful in giving you the time, head space, and tools to make effective choices in difficult situations. STOP is a helpful acronym to remember the steps:

S TOP: Stop what you are doing and freeze your body. Don't say or do anything!

T AKE A STEP BACK: Either literally take one (or more) steps away from the person or situation causing you distress or mentally take a step back by taking a deep breath or giving yourself a break.

O BSERVE: Notice what is happening. In your head, describe the facts, including what is being said and done and what you're thinking and feeling. Based on this information, what are your options?

P ROCEED MINDFULLY: Based on the facts and your goals, act in line with your goals and values. Do what your Wise Mind says.

DBT SKILLS LIST

(Based on the work of Linehan, 2015; Rathus and Miller, 2015)

Refer to this cheat sheet whenever you need a refresher on the DBT skills covered in this book.

WISE MIND *(p. 30)*: Using our emotions and reason to be effective

---

MINDFULNESS *(p. 16)*: Staying in the moment *right now* without judgment

- **What to do:**
  - Wordless observing
  - Describing with words
  - Fully participating

- **How to do it:**
  - Focus on one thing
  - Without judgment
  - Doing what works

DISTRESS TOLERANCE *(p. 33)*: Coping without making things worse

- **Distract with ACCEPTS**
  - **A** ctivities
  - **C** ontributions
  - **C** omparisons
  - **E** motions
  - **P** ush away
  - **T** houghts
  - **S** ensations

- **Self-Soothe**
  - Vision
  - Hearing
  - Smell
  - Taste
  - Touch

- **IMPROVE the Moment**
  - **I**magery
  - **M**eaning
  - **P**rayer
  - **R**elaxation
  - **O**ne thing in the moment
  - **V**acation
  - **E**ncouragement

- **Pros and Cons**

- **TIPP**
  - **T**emperature
  - **I**ntense exercise
  - **P**aced breathing
  - **P**rogressive muscle relaxation

- **STOP**
  - **S**top
  - **T**ake a step back
  - **O**bserve
  - **P**roceed mindfully

- **Radical Acceptance**
  - Turn the Mind
  - Half-smile
  - Willing hands
  - Mindfulness of Breath
  - Acceptance is a choice
  - Mindfulness of Thoughts

EMOTION REGULATION *(p. 55)*: Reducing unwanted emotions and decreasing vulnerabilities

- **ABC PLEASE**
  - **A** ccumulating Short- and Long-Term Positive Experiences
  - **B** uilding Mastery
  - **C** oping Ahead
  - **PLEASE** skills
    - Treat **P** hysica**L** illness.
    - Balance **E** ating.
    - **A** void mood-altering drugs.
    - Balance **S** leep.
    - Get **E** xercise.

- **Check the Facts**

- **Problem-Solving**

- **Opposite Action**

- **Mindfulness of Emotions (the Wave Skill)**

INTERPERSONAL EFFECTIVENESS *(p. 88)*: Increasing effectiveness in our relationships

- **DEAR MAN: Getting what you want/saying no**
  - **D** escribe
  - **E** xpress
  - **A** ssert
  - **R** einforce
  - Be **M** indful
  - **A** ppear Confident
  - **N** egotiate

- **GIVE: Building/Maintaining Relationships**
  - Be **G** entle
  - Act **I** nterested
  - **V** alidate
  - Use an **E** asy Manner

- **FAST: Maintaining Self-Respect**
  - Be **F** air
  - (No) **A** pologies
  - **S** tick to your values/opinions
  - Be **T** ruthful

- **THINK: Giving the Benefit of the Doubt**
  - **T** hink
  - **H** ave empathy
  - **I** nterpretations
  - **N** otice
  - Use **K** indness

- **Mindfulness of Others: Being Present in Our Relationships**

WALKING THE MIDDLE PATH *(p. 110)*: Flexibly balancing change and acceptance in life

- **Dialectics**
  - Opposite truths can both be true; synthesize the kernel of truth in both sides.
  - We are all connected and influence each other.
  - Change is the only constant.

- **Validation of others**
  - Communicating thoughts/feelings/behaviors of others makes sense and is understandable.

- **Coping with invalidation and self-validation**
  - Communicating thoughts/feelings/behaviors of self makes sense and is understandable.

- **Reinforcing effective behaviors in ourselves and others**
  - Positive Reinforcement: Provide rewards
  - Negative Reinforcement: Provide relief
  - Shaping: Reward the small steps toward a larger goal

- **Ignoring ineffective behaviors in ourselves and others**
  - Withhold reinforcers
  - Satiation: Satisfy the function/reinforce before problematic behaviors arise

+1 RULE *(p. 134)*

1. Rate your current distress as a result of the stressful situation on a scale of 0 to 5.

2. Add the number 1 to that number (hence, the +1 Rule).

3. The total number is the number of skills you need to cope with that situation.

Appendix

WORKSHEETS

Here you'll find a weekly tracker, guide to creating a coping kit, and several reusable worksheets. These worksheets are all available for download at dbtteen.zeitgeistpublishing.com so that you can print and reuse them as many times as you'd like. Or, feel free to copy and fill in the prompts in your personal DBT notebook.

DAILY AND/OR WEEKLY DBT SKILLS TRACKER

Record your use of DBT skills on a daily or weekly basis using this tracker.

I reduced vulnerabilities with ABC PLEASE skills:

- [ ] Engaged in a pleasant activity
- [ ] Engaged in one step toward long-term goal
- [ ] Completed a building mastery activity
- [ ] Coped ahead
- [ ] Treated physical illness
- [ ] Enlisted balanced eating
- [ ] Avoided mood-altering drugs and alcohol
- [ ] Got balanced sleep
- [ ] Exercised

- [ ] **I practiced mindfulness**

I avoided making things worse by using:

- [ ] Distract with ACCEPTS
- [ ] Self-Soothing
- [ ] IMPROVE the Moment
- [ ] TIPP
- [ ] STOP

If I had difficult emotions, I used:

- [ ] Check the Facts
- [ ] Problem-Solving
- [ ] Opposite Action
- [ ] Mindfulness of Emotions

I used the following interpersonal effectiveness skills:

- [ ] DEAR MAN to get what I want/say no
- [ ] GIVE to maintain relationships
- [ ] FAST to maintain my self-respect
- [ ] THINK to give the benefit of the doubt
- [ ] Mindfulness of Others to enhance my relationships

I walked the middle path by:

- [ ] Thinking and being dialectical
- [ ] Validating others
- [ ] Validating myself
- [ ] Reinforcing myself
- [ ] Reinforcing others
- [ ] Ignoring my urges/behavior that I want to decrease
- [ ] Ignoring others' behaviors that I want to decrease

CREATE A COPING KIT

Adapted from Distress Tolerance Handout 13 in *DBT Skills Manual for Adolescents* by Jill Rathus and Alec Miller (2015)

Use this chart to make a coping kit for dealing with difficult situations. The coping kit can be a box or bag where you place everything you need to cope with or tolerate difficult situations. Feel free to decorate it! Create a kit to keep at home and a to-go kit for dealing with crises when you are at school, work, or otherwise out and about. Refer to Chapter 2 for ideas. For those strategies that you can't leave in a box (such as your phone to listen to music or talk to friends, ice that would melt, etc.), you can write down reminders of what would be helpful to you. Keep your coping kits easily accessible.

HOME COPING KIT

1. _____ 6. _____

2. _____ 7. _____

3. _____ 8. _____

4. _____ 9. _____

5. _____ 10. _____

ON-THE-GO COPING KIT

1. _____ 6. _____

2. _____ 7. _____

3. _____ 8. _____

4. _____ 9. _____

5. _____ 10. _____

CHECK THE FACTS

Adapted from Emotion Regulation Handout 19 in *DBT Skills Manual for Adolescents*
by Jill Rathus and Alec Miller (2015) and Emotion Regulation Worksheet 5 in
DBT Skills Training Handouts and Worksheets by Marsha Linehan (2015)

1. Emotion I want to change (choose one): _____

    Intensity of the emotion (0–100): _____

    Amount of time I've been feeling this way: _____

2. Describe the situation that is causing the emotion (as if you were
    talking to a friend).

    _____

    _____

    _____

    _____

3. Separate fact from interpretation/assumptions/judgments by
    asking yourself:

    ● Am I correctly interpreting the situation? Are there other
       possible explanations? What is the most likely/effective inter-
       pretation?

       _____

       _____

       _____

- Am I thinking about the situation in extremes (for example, catastrophizing, all-or-nothing thinking, "should" statements)?

  _____

  _____

  _____

- What is the worst that I'm imagining, and what are the chances of that happening?

  _____

  _____

- Even if the worst-case scenario did occur, how could I cope well with it?

  _____

  _____

  _____

4. Based on all this information:

   - Does the emotion fit the facts?   YES   NO
     If no, why? _____

   - Does the intensity fit the facts?   YES   NO
     If no, what is it? (0–100): _____

   - Does the duration fit the facts?   YES   NO
     If no, why? _____

COPE-AHEAD PREP

What's the upcoming situation that you are worried will cause you emotional distress? Describe the facts of the situation. What specific emotions will the situation bring up?

_____

_____

_____

_____

List the DBT skills that will help you cope effectively with this situation. Remember the +1 Rule as a guide to help you identify the number of skills you need to get through this effectively. If one of your skills is using DEAR MAN GIVE FAST interpersonal effectiveness skills, write on the back of the page what you'll say.

1. _____

2. _____

3. _____

4. _____

5. _____

6. _____

Imagine yourself in the situation using the skills you identified. What would you say, think, and do?

_____

_____

_____

_____

As you rehearse the situation in your mind, identify possible obstacles and troubleshoot them.

_____

_____

_____

_____

Keep imagining your successful use of skills until the situation arrives. You can do this!

COMBINING INTERPERSONAL EFFECTIVENESS SKILLS

Planning What to Say and How to Say It

Adapted from Emotion Regulation Handout 19 in DBT Skills Manual for Adolescents by Jill Rathus and Alec Miller (2015) and Emotion Regulation Worksheet 5 in DBT Skills Training Handouts and Worksheets by Marsha Linehan (2015)

Describe the situation that you need to address:

_____

_____

What is your #1 priority in this situation? Rank-order the following:

_____ Getting what you want/saying no

_____ Building/maintaining a relationship

_____ Maintaining your self-respect

How do the following factors affect whether you ask for something/ say no and how strongly to do so:

- Capabilities
- Preparation
- Give and take

- Authority
- Timeliness
- Relationship

- Rights
- Long-term versus short-term goals

_____

_____

_____

Write out what you will say and how you would respond to the other person using these skills:

SKILL	WHEN	WHAT
DEAR MAN	Getting What You Want/Saying No	• **D** escribe • **E** xpress • **A** ssert • **R** einforce • Be **M** indful • **A** ppear Confident • **N** egotiate
GIVE	Building/ Maintaining Relationships	• Be **G** entle • Act **I** nterested • **V** alidate • Use an **E** asy Manner
FAST	Maintaining Self-Respect	• Be **F** air • (No) **A** pologies • **S** tick to Your Values/ Opinions • Be **T** ruthful

RESOURCES

MINDFULNESS APPS

(available for iOS and Android)

- Calm
- Headspace
- Smiling Mind
- Mindfulness Coach

WEBSITES

Free and confidential 24/7 helplines in the US

- 988lifeline.org (call 988 via phone)
- crisistextline.org (text HOME or HELLO to 741741)

Information on DBT and directory of DBT-trained therapists

- behavioraltech.org
- dbt-lbc.org

Information on anxiety and directory of therapists for anxiety

- adaa.org

Guided mindfulness recordings

- cih.ucsd.edu/mindfulness/mindfulness-compassion-resources

Information on DBT skills

- youtube.com/dbtru (videos are in English and several other languages)

BOOKS

For Teens

- *Anxiety Relief for Teens* by Regine Galanti
- *The Dialectical Behavior Therapy Skills Workbook for Anxiety: Breaking Free from Worry, Panic, PTSD, and Other Anxiety Symptoms* by Alexander L. Chapman, Kim L. Gratz, Matthew T. Tull, and Terence Keane
- *The Mindfulness Solution for Intense Emotions: Take Control of Borderline Personality Disorder with DBT* by Cedar R. Koons

For Family Members

- *Parenting a Teen Who Has Intense Emotions: DBT Skills to Help Your Teen Navigate Emotional and Behavioral Challenges* by Pat Harvey and Britt H. Rathbone
- *The Power of Validation* by Karyn D. Hall and Melissa H. Cook

For additional wise mind exercises

- *DBT Skills Training Handouts and Worksheets* by Marsha M. Linehan

For clinicians interested in learning more about DBT

- Linehan, Marsha M. *Cognitive-Behavioral Treatment of Borderline Personality Disorder.* New York: Guilford, 1993.
- Linehan, Marsha M. *DBT Skills Training Handouts and Worksheets* (2nd Ed.). New York: Guilford, 2015.
- Linehan, Marsha M. *DBT Skills Training Manual* (2nd Ed.). New York: Guilford, 2015.
- Miller, Alec L., Jill H. Rathus, and Marsha M. Linehan. *Dialectical Behavior Therapy for Suicidal Adolescents.* New York: Guilford, 2007.
- Rathus, Jill H., and Alec L. Miller. *DBT Skills Manual for Adolescents.* New York: Guilford, 2015.

REFERENCES

Bolt Taylor, Jill. *My Stroke of Insight: A Brain Scientist's Personal Journey.* New York: Penguin, 2006.

Brown, Julie F. *The Emotion Regulation Skills System for Cognitively Challenged Clients: A DBT Informed Approach.* New York: Guilford, 2016.

Dunkley, Christine. "Conceptual and Practical Issues in the Application of Emotion Regulation in Dialectical Behaviour Therapy." In *The Oxford Handbook of Dialectical Behaviour Therapy*, edited by Michaela A. Swales. Oxford, UK: Oxford University Press, 2017 oxfordhandbooks.com.

Lieberman, Matthew D., Naomi I. Eisenberger, Molly J. Crockett, Sabrina M. Tom, Jennifer H. Pfeifer, and Baldwin M. Way. "Putting Feelings into Words: Affect Labeling Disrupts Amgydala Activity in Response to Affective Stimuli." *Psychological Science* 18, 5 (May 2007): 421–28. doi: 10.1111/j.1467-9280.2007.01916.x

Linehan, Marsha M. *Cognitive-Behavioral Treatment of Borderline Personality Disorder.* New York: Guilford, 1993.

Linehan, Marsha M. *DBT Skills Training Handouts and Worksheets* (2nd Ed.). New York: Guilford, 2015.

Linehan, Marsha M. *DBT Skills Training Manual* (2nd Ed.). New York: Guilford, 2015.

Miller, Alec L., Jill H. Rathus, and Marsha M. Linehan. *Dialectical Behavior Therapy for Suicidal Adolescents.* New York: Guilford, 2007.

Moore, Adam, Thomas Gruber, Jennifer Derose, and Peter Malinowski. "Regular, Brief Mindfulness Meditation Practice Improves Electrophysiological Markers of Attentional Control." *Frontiers in Human Neuroscience* 6 (2012). doi: 10.3389/fnhum.2012.00018

Rathus, Jill H., and Alec L. Miller. *DBT Skills Manual for Adolescents*. New York: Guilford, 2015.

Seligman, Martin E.P. *Flourish*. New York: Simon and Schuster, 2011

Swenson, Charles R. *DBT Principles in Action: Acceptance, Change, and Dialectics*. New York: Guilford, 2016.

Watier, Nicholas and Michel Dubois. "The Effects of a Brief Mindfulness Exercise on Executive Attention and Recognition Memory." *Mindfulness* 7 (2016): 745-753. DOI:10.1007/S12671-016-0514-Z

Xu, Mengran, Christine Purdon, Paul Seli, Daniel Smilek. "Mindfulness and Mind Wandering: The Protective Effects of Brief Meditation in Anxious Individuals." *Consciousness and Cognition* 51 (2017): 157-165. doi: 10.1016/j.concog.2017.03.009

INDEX

ACKNOWLEDGMENTS

The DBT skills described in this book are based on the work by Marsha Linehan, Alec Miller, and Jill Rathus. Without their insightfulness and ingenuity, DBT for adolescents would not have been created, and this book could not have been written. I am greatly indebted to each of them for creating a treatment and a set of skills that have helped so many individuals build lives worth living.

To the DBT experts from whom I received formal DBT training and read their written publications, including Shireen Rizvi, Charles Swenson, Kelly Koerner, Alan Fruzzetti, Melanie Harned, Jill Rathus, and Randy Wolbert, as well as the myriad authors of clinically oriented DBT published articles, and members of the DBT-L listserv, you have all influenced how I think about and teach these skills. Together, you have shaped me into a more effective DBT therapist, supervisor, and teacher. Thank you!

Thank you to my editors, Clara Lee and Sarah Curley, for giving me the opportunity to write this book! You provided excellent cheerleading, validation, and reinforcement, for which I am truly grateful!

Thank you to my DBT teams at Trinitas and CCBT. Your cheerleading and assistance with brainstorming was invaluable!

To Essie Larson, you are the best work partner that anyone could ask for! Thank you so much for being my second pair of eyes with this book and reading earlier versions of this manuscript to make sure it was as consistent with DBT as possible.

Thank you to my friends and family for all of their encouragement. To my beloved children, Maayan and Ayelet: You are in a book! Thank you for your unwavering faith that Mommy can write a book; I can't wait to see how you fulfill your dreams! Finally, a huge thanks to my husband, Meir. You are my greatest cheerleader, always encouraging me to take on new and rewarding challenges. This book wouldn't have happened if you hadn't believed I could fit writing into our already hectic life. I love you!

ABOUT THE AUTHOR

ATARA HILLER, PsyD, is a licensed psychologist and a Dialectical Behavior Therapy (DBT)-Linehan Board of Certification (LBC) Certified Clinician. She is co-director of the Trinitas Institute for DBT and Allied Treatments, a DBT-LBC Certified Program, in Elizabeth, New Jersey. In that capacity, Dr. Hiller directs the comprehensive adolescent DBT program, which treats teens and their families with emotion regulation difficulties. She trains and supervises fellow clinicians and psychology graduate students in the practice of DBT, as well as provides individual DBT and leads DBT multifamily skills groups. Dr. Hiller also directs and treats teens and families in an outpatient comprehensive adolescent DBT program at the Center for Cognitive Behavior Therapy, a private practice in East Brunswick, New Jersey. She has extensive experience providing evidence-based treatments to children, adolescents, and adults struggling with anxiety, depression, and symptoms of trauma, as well as complex psychosocial stressors. Dr. Hiller has frequently written about and presented on DBT, borderline personality disorder, suicidality and non-suicidal self-injury, and treatment for child sexual abuse.

Hi there,

We hope *DBT Skills for Teens with Anxiety* helped
you. If you have any questions or concerns about your
book, or have received a damaged copy, please contact
customerservice@penguinrandomhouse.com. We're
here and happy to help.

Also, please consider writing a review on your
favorite retailer's website to let others know what
you thought of the book.

Sincerely,
The Zeitgeist Team